UNJUST ENRICHMENT:

Nathan Tamblyn

MA (Oxford) LLM PhD (Cambridge) Barrister FHEA

Senior Lecturer, University of Exeter Law School

2nd edition 2017

Text & cover photo © 2017 Nathan Tamblyn

To Graham

PREFACE

This book is intended for readers new to the subject of unjust enrichment. It seeks to make it accessible and navigable, by identifying the outline governing principles which structure the modern law. Under each such principle is discussed the case law which supports it, and which provides illustrative detail of how it is applied in practice.

This second edition is revised and updated. It covers the law of England & Wales. (Some reference is made to decisions in other common law jurisdictions.) I have sought to state the law as of 1 March 2017. This book remains dedicated to Professor Graham Virgo, in gratitude for first teaching me this subject.

CONTENTS

PART I – THE CAUSE OF ACTION

CHAPTER 1: INTRODUCTIONS

What is unjust enrichment?

If you pay someone under a contract, and get nothing of what was promised in return; if you give someone a generous gift, but only because they exerted an undue influence over you; if you paid too much tax by mistake – should you get your money back? If the answer is yes, then the mechanism is the law of unjust enrichment.

Unjust enrichment is a cause of action in the law of obligations, on a par with tort law and contract law.

Origins and language

A brief sketch of the pre-history of the law of unjust enrichment is important to understand some of the language still found in books and judgments.[1]

Anyone bringing a modern law suit must issue a Claim Form, the formal document which starts court proceedings. In it, the claimant must plead all the relevant facts, and what remedy they want. They do not plead the law: which legal principles apply to resolve the dispute will be a matter for advocacy and discussion before the court. That said, it is usually obvious whether the claim alleges, for example, breach of contract, or the tort of negligence.

---

[1] See: Baker 1998

13

Before the modern age, bringing a claim used to be much more formulaic. There were 'forms of action': in effect, standard form documents which allowed a party to bring certain types of complaint, but not others. It mattered that the claimant chose the correct form of action. If the claimant chose incorrectly, the claim might be thrown out – even if the complaint was otherwise meritorious. Also, different forms of action entailed different processes, and some might prove more convenient to a claimant than others.

We no longer have the forms of action, but the early development of the law of unjust enrichment was constrained by them.

So once upon a time, there was a legal complaint called 'action on the case upon assumpsit'. Two particular forms were 'quantum meruit', where services were performed without an agreed price, and 'quantum valebant', where goods were sold without an agreed price. The claimant would allege that the defendant had requested the goods or services, and had promised to pay whatever was deserved. Sometimes the defendant did indeed expressly promise to pay the claimant 'whatever was deserved'. At any rate, an implied promise to pay *something* could usually be identified from the facts. It was for the court to decide how much should be paid.

Another form of assumpsit was called 'indebitatus assumpsit'. It rested upon the convoluted claim that the defendant, already being indebted to the claimant, and in consideration of that debt continuing, had promised a second time to repay it. In other words, not only had the defendant promised to repay the debt at the outset of the transaction, but there was supposedly a second re-promise to repay, after the transaction was already on foot.

This second promise was almost always a fiction: the defendant almost never made any such second promise explicitly. Instead, the law simply implied the promise. This was necessary to squeeze the facts of any dispute within the assumpsit formula. Otherwise, the claimant would have had to sue upon the original promise, and that might mean using a different form of action (a writ of debt, instead of assumpsit).

When using indebitatus assumpsit, it was necessary for the claimant to indicate why the defendant was indebted to him: for 'money had and received' (eg a loan), or for work done, or for goods sold – together, these indications were known as the 'common counts'.

The common count of money had and received was developed to include situations where the claimant paid money to the defendant by mistake. The claim stated simply that the defendant was indebted to the claimant in the amount paid, and that the defendant had promised (but failed) to repay it. No doubt in most cases the defendant should have repaid the money received by mistake, but the plea of an implied *promise* to repay was again pure fiction – the defendant never made any such promise.

The common count of money had and received was then developed still further to include situations where the claimant's payment had been compelled, or had been made under a void contract, or under a contract whose consideration had totally failed. This was now a long way from a simple loan.

15

The position was encapsulated in a judgment of Lord Mansfield from 1760:

> If the defendant be under an obligation, from the ties of natural justice, to refund; the law implies a debt, and gives this action [assumpsit for money had and received], founded in the equity of the plaintiff's case, as it were upon a contract ('quasi ex contractu'…).[2]

This pre-history continues to exert its influence. Reference can still be found to implied promises, implied contracts, and quasi-contract.

However, the implied contract theory has now been judicially disapproved at the highest level,[3] and rightly so. It was a relic of ancient pleading practices and litigation processes long since gone; there is no need for any modern claimant to squeeze his claim into any particular form. And it was a fictional account, objectionable on that basis alone, and which obscured the principled development of unjust enrichment as a cause of action in its own right.

Indeed, unjust enrichment is even available when it is not possible to imply a contract because, for example, the defendant lacks the capacity to enter such contracts.[4]

---

[2] *Moses v Macferlan* (1760) 2 Burr 1005, 1008; 97 ER 676, 678

[3] *Westdeutsche Landesbank Girozentrale v Islington London Borough Council* [1996] AC 669, 710; *Benedetti v Sawiris* [2013] UKSC 50, [148]

[4] *Haugesund Kommune v Depfa ACS Bank* [2010] EWCA Civ 579

And yet the language of the common counts is still used by modern lawyers, albeit as shorthand for the type of claim being brought. So 'money had and received' is shorthand for 'I paid money and now I want it back';[5] and 'quantum meruit' means 'I have given you services and now I want money for them'; and 'quantum valebant' means 'I have given you goods and now I want money for them'.

Unjust enrichment was recognized as a cause of action in England only as late as 1991.[6] Its history has not been linear. The law has tried various approaches. Over time, some approaches were discarded, some evolved, others blended together, and we have ended up where we are, almost by trial and error, but according to a very particular and conscientious process of trial and error. It is important now to stake out a modern and straightforward account of the law of unjust enrichment. Of course it will be informed by the past. But there is little need to re-invent old cases, from a time before the recognition of unjust enrichment, subjecting them to concepts and language they did not use and did not have available. Since its recognition, unjust enrichment has proved a popular cause of action, and there is now enough modern precedent to anchor a modern statement of the law.

---

[5] For example, *South Tyneside Metropolitan Borough Council v Svenska International plc* [1995] 1 All ER 545, 557 confirms that 'money had and received' means that the underlying cause of action is unjust enrichment. See too: *Shanghai Tongji Science and Technology Industrial Co Ltd v Casil Clearing Ltd* (2004) 7 HKCFAR 79, [66]; *Cheong Shing Ltd v Yu Kwan* (2008) 11 HKCFAR 594, [54].

[6] *Lipkin Gorman v Karpnale Ltd* [1991] 2 AC 548, although, ironically, that case might itself be best seen, not as an example of unjust enrichment, but rather as a claim in property law. But endorsing its unjust enrichment analysis, see: *Re Hampton Capital Ltd* [2015] EWHC 1905 (Ch).

Compensation and restitution

Compensation measures loss in the hands of the claimant. Restitution measures gain in the hands of the defendant.

In contract law, for example, the usual measure of damages is compensatory: the innocent party is compensated for his expectation loss, ie the shortfall he suffered because the promise made to him was broken. Restitution can be awarded in contract law, but only exceptionally, and at the discretion of the court, where the usual remedies in contract law are inadequate, and where the victim has a legitimate interest in preventing the profit-earning activity of the party in breach.[7]

However, restitution is the principal remedy when unjust enrichment is the cause of action: the defendant has to pay back the enrichment he made unjustly at the expense of the claimant.

There used to be discussion about whether unjust enrichment and restitution are the same things or different things. Many people used the terms interchangeably. The better approach, and standard modern practice, is to call the remedy restitution and the cause of action unjust enrichment. But it pays to ascertain which meaning is intended, especially in some of the older books and judgments.

---

[7] *AG v Blake* [2001] 1 AC 268

Because unjust enrichment is concerned with restitution, not compensation, the claimant is under no duty to mitigate his loss, and there is no defence of 'passing on'.[8] The latter is best explained with an example:

A defendant wholesaler charges £100 too much to the claimant retailer, who mistakenly pays the full amount. But to compensate, the claimant puts up the prices to his customers by £110. On discovering his mistake, the claimant can still claim £100 back from the defendant in unjust enrichment. It is no defence that the claimant is no longer out of pocket, having passed on the loss to his customers.

This is unsurprising. To repeat, restitution concerns gains in the hands of the defendant. It is not concerned whether the claimant has suffered any loss at all. Put simply, the £100 was not the defendant's to keep. He got it by mistake and should give it back. That is unaffected by whatever the claimant did subsequently.

Contract law and unjust enrichment

What is the relationship between the law of unjust enrichment and contract law? It is essential to understand this. To paraphrase Langbein, the law of unjust enrichment is historically contingent upon the rest of the law of obligations, and especially contract; only once the contours of the modern law of contract are worked out is it possible to see the range of problems left to be solved by unjust enrichment.[9]

---

[8] *Kleinwort Benson Ltd v Birmingham City Council* [1997] QB 380

[9] Langbein 1998: 59

There is still a strong relationship between contract law and unjust enrichment. Duress, undue influence, and unconscionable conduct can vitiate a contract; they are also recognized unjust factors in the law of unjust enrichment. Mistake and misrepresentation can vitiate a contract; mistake is a recognized unjust factor (including those induced mistakes which would otherwise be called misrepresentation in contract law). A total failure to perform what was promised is a repudiatory breach of contract; that scenario also engages the unjust factor 'failure of basis'.

This overlap between contract and unjust enrichment is no doubt partly a legacy of the fact that the principles of unjust enrichment were developed latently within the confines of implied or quasi-contract (see above). Regardless, it should not be surprising that conduct condemned and remedied in one area of law similarly finds remedies in other areas too. For example, tort law also recognizes pleas of duress (in the form of the cause of action called intimidation) and misrepresentation.

However, there is good reason why there *must* be this overlap between contract law and unjust enrichment.

For example, if a contract is void for mistake, but money has already been paid under the void contract, how can the payer get his money back? Not through contract law: there is by definition no contract upon which to bring a claim. The payer must bring his claim in unjust enrichment. So mistake operates in contract law to render a contract void, and it operates in unjust enrichment to enable the payer to recover any money paid over.

It is the same with misrepresentation, duress, undue influence, and unconscionable conduct, which are vitiating factors in contract law which render a contract voidable and so liable to rescission. Contract law determines whether or not the contract should be rescinded. Once a contract is rescinded, contract law is spent. In effect, by providing a remedy of rescission, contract law has disabled itself from doing any more. This is because rescission cancels the contract. Past and future obligations are erased. It is as if the contract never happened. Without a contract, there is no basis upon which contract law could provide for restitution.

If the innocent party wishes to obtain restitution, ie recover anything he has paid out, under the rescinded contract, that is a matter for unjust enrichment. The rescission of the contract has cleared the ground for a claim in unjust enrichment by removing any defence (see below). Then it is simply a question of asking whether the defendant has been enriched, at the expense of the claimant, through one or more of the recognized unjust factors – which will likely include the unjust factor (in unjust enrichment) which corresponds to the vitiating factor (in contract law) which rendered the contract voidable in the first place.[10]

Nevertheless, unjust enrichment is also broader than the shadow of contract law. Restitutionary damages are an exceptional remedy in contract law, but restitution is available as of right in unjust enrichment. Further, the unjust factor 'failure of basis' applies not just to unfulfilled promises, but also to unfulfilled legitimate expectations which fall short of contract (see chapter 8). What is more, money can be recovered in unjust enrichment in situations beyond

---

[10] See: Tamblyn 2016

contract: for example, when it was paid under legal compulsion (chapter 9), or in consequence of a public authority receiving a payment which was not lawfully due (chapter 10). Unjust enrichment can also be pleaded when the transaction was one of gift.[11]

So unjust enrichment has an important role to play as a supplement to contract law, and often it must engage with contract law to clear the ground for its own claim, but it cannot be tied solely to contract law. The techniques used in unjust enrichment must be broader.

---

[11] *Allcard v Skinner* (1887) 36 Ch D 145; *Re Glubb* [1900] 1 Ch 354; *Clarke v Prus* [1995] NPC 41

Elements of the cause of action

1.1 A claimant in unjust enrichment must prove: (i) that the defendant has been enriched; (ii) at the expense of the claimant; (iii) through a recognised unjust factor. There is then a question (iv) of defences.

This approach has been endorsed in a number of cases.[12] If successful, the claimant will obtain restitution, ie he will recover, in money, the enrichment which the defendant made at his expense.

Note that it is not every injustice which sounds in unjust enrichment. Similarly, not every unreasonable conduct sounds in tort, and not every promise results in a contract. Unjust enrichment only applies to recognized types of injustice, those which are sufficiently serious as to warrant the intervention of the law. The recognised unjust factors are explored in Part II below.

The presence of an unjust factor is essential. Enrichment on its own is not sufficient. Thus a claimant cannot claim restitution from a defendant who happens to benefit incidentally from an activity voluntarily carried on by the claimant.

---

[12] *Banque Financiere de la Cite v Parc (Battersea) Ltd* [1999] 1 AC 221, 227; *Benedetti v Sawiris* [2013] UKSC 50, [10]; *Bank of Cyprus UK Ltd v Menelaou* [2015] UKSC 66. On the need to prove the presence of an unjust factor, rather than relying on Birks' 'absence of basis' approach, see: *Deutsche Morgan Grenfell Group plc v IRC* [2007] 1 AC 558, [21]; *Test Claimants in the FII Group Litigation v HMRC* [2012] UKSC 19, [81], [188]. (Note that absence of basis is not to be confused with failure of basis.)

CHAPTER 2: ENRICHMENT

Defendant enriched

2.1 The claimant must show that the defendant has been enriched.

What counts as enrichment can be broad and inclusive, and is largely a matter of common sense.

Enrichment can include the receipt of money or goods, sometimes called positive enrichment, or positive benefit. In fact, when a party receives money, they are often doubly enriched: first, by the lump sum itself, and second, by the 'use value' of the money, ie the amount of interest saved on an equivalent loan.[13] Thus enrichment can also be a saved expense, sometimes called negative enrichment, or negative benefit. This can include paying off a debt,[14] or when the other side foregoes a civil claim.[15]

It is just as important to identify when a party is not enriched.

Consider the following example. Pursuant to a contract, A delivers goods to B on credit. B owes £100. B later pays £100. But B paid this by mistake (he

---

[13] *Sempra Metals Ltd v Inland Revenue Commissioners* [2007] UKHL 34. On how to quantify that use value, see: *Littlewoods Ltd v Revenue and Customs Commissioners* [2015] EWCA Civ 515, [195]-[197].

[14] *Filby v Mortgage Express (No 2) Ltd* [2004] EWCA Civ 759

[15] *Gibb v Maidstone and Tunbridge Wells NHS Trust* [2008] EWCA Civ 678, [30]

meant to pay someone else instead). Surely B should not be able to recover the money from A.[16]

One answer is that A is not enriched. Yes, he has received money. But this is cancelled out in one of two ways.

First, we can say that A has given consideration in return. In other words, he has swapped the money for the goods. (It could have been services. Or perhaps an enforceable promise.) His net position is unchanged.

Further, B cannot say that A remains enriched on account of some supposed disparity between the money and the consideration. This is because contract law will not embark on any exercise which judges the adequacy of consideration.[17] In other words, it assumes that consideration is adequate to the price. Alternatively, the fact that B agreed the contract price would estopp him from denying the adequacy.

Second, as Edelman and Bant originally put it,[18] we might say that a person in A's position is never enriched because he merely exchanges one asset (the contractual right to payment) for another asset (the payment itself). Similarly, a bank is not enriched when it receives money for the account of one of its clients: this is because that receipt is matched by a liability to pay the money back out to the client.[19]

---

[16] *Fairfield Sentry Ltd v Migani* [2014] UKPC 9, [18]

[17] *Chappell & Co Ltd v Nestle Co Ltd* [1960] AC 87

[18] Edelman and Bant 2006: 345

[19] *Jeremy D Stone Consultants Ltd v National Westminster Bank plc* [2013] EWHC 208 (Ch); *Challinor v Juliet Bellis & Co* [2015] EWCA Civ 59

Objective valuation

2.2 Enrichment is valued objectively, at the time of receipt.

Enrichment is to be valued objectively. This is usually the market price, except that the defendant's status might raise or lower that objective market price;[20] for example, a party with a strong bargaining position might be able to negotiate more favourable terms.

Enrichment is to be valued at the time when the goods or services were received, and the enrichment will be the value of the services themselves, not any end product or subsequent profit.[21]

What happens when a price was specified in a contract (now void or rescinded)? Does it set a ceiling on the valuation? There are cases going both ways.[22] The better position, as a matter of principle, is that the contract price may be evidence of objective value, but need not decide the matter conclusively.

---

[20] *Benedetti v Sawiris* [2013] UKSC 50

[21] *Benedetti v Sawiris* [2013] UKSC 50, [14]

[22] *Taylor v Motability Finance Ltd* [2004] EWHC 2619 (Comm), [26] (ceiling); *Rover International Ltd v Cannon Film Sales Ltd (No 3)* [1989] 3 All ER 423 (no ceiling)

Subjective devaluation

2.3 The defendant is not enriched by the receipt of something which he can subjectively devalue.

An objective benefit is something which a reasonable person would consider a benefit, or something with a market value. But the defendant may 'subjectively devalue' what he has received if he personally does not see it as a benefit.

For example, the defendant might be given a DVD, which has an objective value, but the defendant may so dislike the film that he personally subjectively devalues it to zero (he would never have bought it).

In the law of unjust enrichment, the defendant is not enriched, and should not have to pay for, something which has merely an objective value (for someone else), but no subjective value for himself, and which has been forced upon him.

Allowing subjective devaluation is thus about protecting the defendant's autonomy.[23] 'Liabilities are not to be forced upon people behind their backs any more than you can confer a benefit upon a man against his will.'[24]

---

[23] *Benedetti v Sawiris* [2013] UKSC 50, [18]

[24] *Falcke v Scottish Imperial Insurance Co* (1886) 34 Ch D 234, 248

Overcoming subjective devaluation

2.4 A plea of subjective devaluation can be challenged by showing that: (i) the receipt was an incontrovertible benefit; or (ii) the defendant's behaviour demonstrates that he values the receipt after all.

The defendant's claim of subjective devaluation is merely evidence like any other, whose weight and credibility needs to be assessed. The claimant can advance counter evidence or arguments to show that the defendant did value the receipt after all.[25]

As for (i):

A defendant cannot credibly deny that he has been enriched if he receives something which is an 'incontrovertible benefit'. For example, money is usually incontrovertibly beneficial. So too is anything that can be converted into money (ie sold). Also, the discharge of one's legal liability (see chapter 9). A service rendered, which one would inevitably have had to pay somebody else to do, is probably also an incontrovertible benefit.[26]

As for (ii):

It is sometimes said that a defendant cannot subjectively devalue that which he has 'freely accepted'.[27] But that proceeds too quickly. For example, a

---

[25] *Benedetti v Sawiris* [2013] UKSC 50, [25]

[26] *Craven-Ellis v Canons Ltd* [1936] 2 KB 403, 412 (managing director); *Re Berkeley Applegate (Investment Consultants) Ltd* [1989] Ch 32, 50 (liquidator)

[27] *Benedetti v Sawiris* [2013] UKSC 50, [25]

party might happily accept the provision of services only if he reasonably believed them to be free (he would not have accepted them at all if he thought payment was due).[28] But it is a different matter, of course, if the defendant could have rejected a service which he would ordinarily expect to pay for, but kept quiet about it until afterwards, hoping to get away with it for free; that smacks of unjust enrichment.

It should not count against the defendant that he 'freely accepted' the receipt of something which he had little chance to reject.[29] 'One cleans another's shoes; what can the other do but put them on?'[30] Or more accurately, and less elegantly, if one man cleans another's shoes, against that other's wishes, and without the other having the opportunity to reject the cleaning, then that other can put the shoes on all the same, and seek to subjectively devalue the cleaning service, perhaps even to zero.

However, other behaviour might demonstrate that the defendant valued the receipt after all. For example, in one case, the defendant was sold a car only, but accidentally he was also given its private number plate. The defendant said the number plate was of no value, but he refused to give it back. The court held that the defendant had to pay for it.[31]

But even here, note that there is a difference between an active choice (like refusing to return) and mere indifference (not bothering to return). Why, in other circumstances, should the defendant have the burden of actively returning

---

[28] *Rowe v Vale of White Horse DC* [2003] EWHC 388 (Admin)

[29] *Chief Constable of Greater Manchester Police v Wigan AFC Ltd* [2008] EWCA Civ 1449

[30] *Taylor v Laird* (1856) 25 LJ Ex 320, 332

[31] *Cressman v Coys of Kensington* [2004] EWCA Civ 47

what was sent to him unsolicited? Surely the burden should be on the sender to retrieve the item? But if the recipient refuses to let the sender even collect the item, again that suggests that he does value it after all.

Restitution is concerned with gains in the hands of the defendant. Subjective devaluation seeks to value correctly what is in the hands of the defendant. But conceptually, it is only one side of the coin. The other side is subjective revaluation. It may be that what the defendant received he valued above any market price. However, it has been held that there is little, if any, scope for subjective revaluation, on the basis that it is not a concept necessary to protect the defendant's freedom of choice.[32]

---

[32] *Benedetti v Sawiris* [2013] UKSC 50, [29]

CHAPTER 3: AT THE EXPENSE OF

Enriched at claimant's expense

3.1 The defendant must be enriched at the expense of the claimant.

This requirement can be expressed in another way, by saying that there must be a transfer of value from the claimant to the defendant. The requirement that the defendant must be enriched at the expense of the claimant does much of the work done in tort and contract by other doctrines like privity and proximity and remoteness.

Some examples might be given of how 'at the expense of' operates.

First, the claimant mistakenly gives the defendant £100, which the defendant then gambles on horse racing and wins. The claimant can recover the £100, but not the winnings. The winnings were not at the claimant's expense; the winnings were not transferred by the claimant. The winnings came from someone else (the bookie). The only transfer of value was the £100.[33]

Second, the defendant owns a locked cabinet which contains valuable treasures, but there is no key. The claimant locksmith makes a key, and the treasures are recovered. In the absence of a contract, the claimant can recover the value of his services in unjust enrichment. But the claimant cannot recover a share of the treasures, which the defendant already owned.

---

[33] Burrows 2011: 66

Similarly, where the claimant procures planning permission in respect of the defendant's property, the claimant is entitled to be paid for his services, but he gets no share of the increased value of the property. The defendant already owned the property, including its development potential value; the planning permission merely unlocked that value.[34]

So too where A repairs B's car, A can recover the cost of repairs, but not a share in the increased value of the car.[35]

Indirect enrichment and leapfrogging

Discussion in the previous section is often couched in terms of 'direct' enrichment. Whereas some cases have also countenanced the idea that a claim might lie where the defendant receives the enrichment indirectly from the claimant.[36] All this requires caution.

Let us start with leapfrogging. Suppose that A transacts with B who transacts with C. The goods or services flow down the chain. If A goes unpaid, obviously A can sue B for breach of contract. But can A leapfrog B to sue C in unjust enrichment?

---

[34] *Yeoman's Row Management Ltd v Cobbe* [2008] UKHL 55, [41]

[35] *Greenwood v Bennett* [1973] QB 195

[36] *Investment Trust Companies v Revenue and Customs Commissioners* [2012] EWHC 458 (Ch), on appeal [2015] EWCA Civ 82; *TFL Management Services v Lloyd's TSB Bank plc* [2013] EWCA Civ 1415 (but see 4.2 below); *Relfo Ltd v Varsani* [2014] EWCA Civ 360; *Bank of Cyprus UK Ltd v Menelaou* [2015] UKSC 66

Leapfrogging might be possible in a number of situations:

First, A might be able to rely upon the laws of agency. But this can avail a claimant across a number of causes of action, and is nothing unique to unjust enrichment.

Second, A might have a proprietary remedy which follows his property into the hands of C; or A might invoke the rules of tracing. But this has nothing to do with unjust enrichment either (see chapter 16).

Third, C might have committed some wrong against A which entitles A to sue him directly. This might allow for restitutionary remedies, but again it takes the matter outside of unjust enrichment, for example into tort or equity.

Fourth, the remedy of subrogation might put A into B's shoes and thus in a position to sue C. Subrogation is a niche topic, and we return to it later (chapter 16).

Otherwise, the courts have repeatedly recognized a general rule against leapfrogging in unjust enrichment, insisting that the parties must be in a direct relationship.[37] This seems fair:

For a start, why should C be liable twice over, once in contract to B, and again in unjust enrichment to A? If C pays A in unjust enrichment, what defence

---

[37] *Colonial Bank v Exhange Bank of Yarmouth* (1885) 11 App Cas 84, 85; *Brown and Davis v Galbraith* [1972] 1 WLR 997 (CA); *Kleinwort Benson Ltd v Birmingham City Council* [1996] 4 All ER 733, 749, on appeal at [1999] 2 AC 349; *Pan Ocean Shipping Co Ltd v Creditcorp, The Trident Beauty* [1994] 1 WLR 161 (HL); *Lloyd's Bank plc v Independent Insurance Co Ltd* [2000] QB 110 (CA); *Uren v First National Home Finance Ltd* [2005] EWHC 2529 (Ch); *Armstrong DLW GmbH v Winnington Networks Ltd* [2012] EWHC 10 (Ch), [97]

would C have against B's claim in contract? What if C has already paid B? Must C pay a second time to A? And if C only bought the goods on the terms agreed with B, why should he be liable on potentially different terms to A?

Further, if B is insolvent, the liquidators would collect in what B is owed, including any payment due from C, and divide the sum equally between the creditors, including A. Why should A sidestep that, and by suing C directly, take priority over other creditors and recover its whole debt, not just a fair share?[38] What would stop every other creditor from trying to do the same?

Fortunately, there are techniques which preclude some of these undesirable outcomes. For example, C might be able to invoke the defence of change of position (see chapter 11): as a consequence of accepting receipt, C has changed its position, by paying, or incurring a liability to pay, under the B / C contract.[39]

Further, the cases in which the concept of indirect enrichment have arisen for discussion are not convincingly cases of indirect enrichment after all. In particular, we need to distinguish between people acting as principals, and people acting as intermediaries:

Consider this example. I give you a book for a birthday present. You do not like the book. So next week, you re-gift it, as another birthday present, to your friend. Here we have two separate transactions. You are clearly acting as a principal. The gift to your friend is from you. If instead, I give you a book, as a

---

[38] *Yew Sang Hong Ltd v Hong Kong Housing Authority* [2008] 3 HKC 290

[39] *Yukio Takahashi v Cheng Zhen Shu* (2011) 14 HKCFAR 558, [38]-[40]

birthday present for your friend, asking you to pass it on to her, and you do, you are clearly acting as an intermediary. The gift to your friend is from me.

Thus, if A sends B a cheque through the post, it is surely a direct payment, even if the letter goes through the Post Office, and any number of intermediaries handle it; so too if A transfers money to B via a series of bank accounts.[40]

If customer X repays money to bank Y, and Y then loans the money to customer Z, there is a direct transfer of value from Y to Z. So too, if instead, Y tells X, out of convenience, to pay the money straight to Z; that is surely a proximate transaction between Y and Z, albeit through the intermediary of X.[41]

Although controversy remains, the better position is probably as follows:

There must be a transfer of value from the claimant to the defendant. This will continue to be the case even where the claimant effects payment through intermediaries. It will cease to be the case where there is an intervening party acting as a principal.

<u>Further examples from the case law</u>

- Charterers A hired a ship from owners B who assigned the right to receive hire to credit agency C. A made advance hire payments to C. The ship went off-hire while undergoing repairs, and could not return to service thereafter. A sought to recover the hire from C. The court held

---

[40] The better explanation of *Relfo Ltd v Varsani* [2014] EWCA Civ 360. See too: *Shanghai Tongji Science and Technology Industrial Co Ltd v Casil Clearing Ltd* (2004) 7 HKCFAR 79

[41] The better explanation of *Bank of Cyprus UK Ltd v Menelaou* [2015] UKSC 66

that A could only recover under the charter party from B. C was entitled to the hire under the B / C contract on terms which precluded any recourse by A.[42]

- Builders A contracted with company B, whose sole shareholders and directors were C, to build houses on C's land. A carried out work, but did not get paid in full. A could only sue B under the contract. A could not circumvent that by suing C in unjust enrichment. A had taken the risk of looking to B for payment (and hence also the risk of B's insolvency).[43]

- Company A won a tender to build and operate a toll road. A contracted with B who contracted with C, and D as an undisclosed joint venture partner. Down the chain flowed the right to participate in the project. Up the chain flowed the obligation to invest. D made out a cashier's order naming A as payee, and handed it over to C, who passed it to B, who passed it to A. When ultimately the contractual chain broke down, D could not recover the money from A. A had not received the cashier's order 'at the expense of' D. Although it named A as payee, it was paid by D to C in order to discharge D's obligations to C, a process repeated at each stage up the chain. And as each recipient took the cashier's order in turn, they gave good consideration for it, or changed their position, by discharging their counter-party to that extent of their obligations.[44] (In

[42] *Pan Ocean Shipping Ltd. v Creditcorp Ltd, The Trident Beauty* [1994] 1 All ER 470, 475

[43] *MacDonald Dickens & Macklin v Costello* [2011] EWCA Civ 930

other words, each intervening party acted as principal, not mere intermediary.)

---

[44] *Yukio Takahashi v Cheng Zhen Shu* (2011) 14 HKCFAR 558

PART II – UNJUST FACTORS

CHAPTER 4: MISTAKE

Actionable mistake

4.1 Any causative mistake is actionable in unjust enrichment.

Mistake in unjust enrichment has a much wider meaning than mistake in contract law. You cannot set aside a contract simply because you made a mistake in entering into it. Contracts are there for certainty. It takes a very particular type of mistake to merit undoing that certainty. But where there is no contract, then why not make restitution for any mistake? After all, the recipient is otherwise protected by defences like change of position (see chapter 11). Beyond that, any money paid by mistake is simply not the recipient's to keep. It should be paid back. Thus the type of mistake needed to support a claim in unjust enrichment can be wider than the type of mistake needed to set aside a contract.[45]

Note further that mistake in contract law has a narrower meaning (covering common mistake and unilateral mistake), while mistake in unjust enrichment has a wider meaning to include the 'induced mistake' of misrepresentation.

A mistake is an incorrect conscious belief, or an incorrect tacit assumption; it is not ignorance.[46] The mistake must have caused the claimant to make the payment.[47]

---

[45] *Midland Bank plc v Brown Shipley & Co Ltd* [1991] 2 All ER 690, 700-701

[46] *Pitt v Holt* [2013] UKSC 26, [108], a case of mistaken gift by deed

Examples from the case law

- The claimant company entered into a contract under which it paid advances to the defendant, and received from the defendant films to dub and distribute, in return for a share in the gross earnings of the films. The contract was void because the claimant was not incorporated at the time, but both parties mistakenly thought the contract was valid. The claimant could recover its payments, and receive a sum to reflect its services in dubbing and distribution.[48]

- The defendant bought a car at auction. By mistake, and contrary to what was said expressly at the auction, the personalized number plate was also transferred to the defendant, but he refused to return the number plate. Because he was unjustly enriched by its receipt, he was obliged to pay for it.[49]

- A delivered his car to B for a service, but B drove the car, crashed it, and then sold it to C. The car was a virtual wreck, and C spent £226 repairing it, before selling it to D. A could recover the car because he retained title. But C could recover (from A) the cost of repairing the car which he mistakenly thought was his.[50]

---

[47] *Barclays Bank Ltd v WJ Simms, Son and Cooke (Southern) Ltd* [1980] QB 677, 695; *Deutsche Morgan Grenfell Group plc v Inland Revenue Commissioners* [2006] UKHL 49, [143]

[48] *Rover International Ltd v Cannon Film Sales Ltd (No 3)* [1989] 3 All ER 423

[49] *Cressman v Coys of Kensington* [2004] EWCA Civ 47

Risk

4.2 Actionable mistake is to be distinguished from risk, mis-prediction and doubt.

Actionable mistake concerns current matters. There is no claim in unjust enrichment if the claimant has instead made a mis-prediction about what might happen in the future.[51] Nor if the claimant had doubts or suspicions that he was probably mistaken.[52]

Any payer who relies upon a prediction of the future, or who acts despite his doubt, is taking a risk. Virgo says that risk-taking is a bar to unjust enrichment.[53] Indeed, it would not be risk-taking at all if the risk was guaranteed to be hedged by restitution in unjust enrichment.

Rather, the law of unjust enrichment will not allow itself to be used such that one party *transfers* the risk to its counter-party. For if a claimant makes a risky payment to the defendant, but can then recover it, effectively unjust enrichment would have transferred the risk from the claimant to the defendant. As a matter of first principles, it seems more appropriate that the payer accepts the

---

[50] *Greenwood v Bennett* [1973] QB 195

[51] *Pitt v Holt* [2013] UKSC 26, [104]; *Patel's Wall Street Exchange Ltd v SK International* [2005] 2 HKLRD 551; *Dextra Bank & Trust Co Ltd v Bank of Jamaica* [2002] 1 All ER (Comm) 193, [29]

[52] *Marine Trade SA v Pioneer Freight Futures Co Ltd BVI* [2009] EWHC 2656 (Comm), [77]

[53] Virgo 2009: 479, 504-506; Virgo 2015: 36-37

consequences of his risky payment, rather than the payee, at least where the payee is unaware of the risk.

So for example, if the claimant supplies a service for free because it is unsure whether it can charge at all, it cannot later seek retrospective payment in restitution; in the meantime, it has run the risk of not getting paid.[54] Similarly, where the claimant paid tolls which were not due, doubting that they were due, and paying under protest, but doing so in order to avoid litigation, that too was not a payment under mistake.[55] More generally, paying, despite doubt, to settle a dispute or to close the transaction, is not a mistake.[56] Also, if litigation is unsuccessful, surely the costs were not incurred by mistake, but pursuant to the inherent risks of litigation.[57]

Similarly, if I make a donation to charity, believing I am rich when I am not, that is a mistake. But if I am rich, and make a donation to charity thinking that I will not need the money, but then lose all my wealth overnight, there is no mistake, only a mis-prediction as to the future.

---

[54] *Rowe v Vale of White Horse DC* [2003] EWHC 388 (Admin)

[55] *Maskell v Horner* [1915] 3 KB 106

[56] *BP Oil International Ltd v Target Shipping Ltd* [2012] EWHC 1590 (Comm), [232], reversed on a different point [2013] EWCA Civ 196

[57] The better explanation for *TFL Management Services v Lloyd's TSB Bank plc* [2013] EWCA Civ 1415

Strict liability

4.3 Mistake is usually strict liability (subject to defences). The payer can recover his payment despite being at fault himself, and despite the payee not knowing of the mistake.

For example, the claimant agreed to buy a house from the defendant, as part of buying the defendant's business, on the basis of non-fraudulent misrepresentations by the defendant as to the value of the business. The claimant could rescind the purchase contract and recover his deposit. It did not matter that the claimant was negligent in appraising himself of the value of the defendant's business.[58]

In another case, A wrote a cheque to B builders. A then told its bank C to stop the cheque. But C paid anyway by mistake. C could recover the money from B, despite C's fault in paying out, and despite B's ignorance of the mistake.[59] (But a payee's *knowledge* of the mistake could preclude a defence of change of position – see chapter 11.)

---

[58] *Redgrave v Hurd* (1881) 20 Ch D 1; see too *Kelly v Solari* (1841) 9 M & W 54, 152 ER 24; *Barclays Bank Ltd v WJ Simms, Son and Cooke (Southern) Ltd* [1980] QB 677

[59] *Barclays Bank Ltd v WJ Simms Ltd* [1980] QB 677; see too *Kelly v Solari* (1841) 9 M & W 54; but contrast *Lloyd's Bank plc v Independent Insurance Co Ltd* [2000] QB 110, where the payee had a defence.

Mistake of law

4.4 Mistake of law in general is actionable. But the better view is that mistake as to the law of unjust enrichment is not actionable.

Money paid under a mistake of law can in general be recovered.

For example, a claimant bank made payments to the defendant councils under interest rate swap agreements. A subsequent House of Lords decision held that such agreements were void for being outside the defendant's powers. The claimant was held entitled to recover the payments as made under mistake of law. It was no defence that payment was made under a previously settled understanding of the law subsequently departed from by judicial decision.[60]

So too, restitution can be sought in respect of tax paid under a regime later held to be unlawful.[61] And restitution can be sought for the value of services provided, when the court subsequently rules that the original basis on which the parties expected the service provider to be paid was unlawful.[62]

We turn now to the unsatisfactory case of *Nurdin & Peacock plc v DB Ramsden & Co Ltd*.[63] The defendant landlord charged more rent than was due. The claimant tenant paid 5 instalments before receiving legal advice that confirmed the

---

[60] *Kleinwort Benson Ltd v Lincoln City Council* [1999] 2 AC 349

[61] *Deutsche Morgan Grenfell Group plc v Inland Revenue Commissioners* [2006] UKHL 49; *Sempra Metals Ltd v Inland Revenue Commissioners* [2007] UKHL 34

[62] *Barnes v Eastenders Cash and Carry plc* [2014] UKSC 26

[63] [1999] 1 All ER 941

defendant was charging too much. That advice was correct. So the claimant could recover those 5 instalments because they were paid in the mistaken belief that they were due.

But the claimant paid another 5 instalments pending trial, to avoid any risk of forfeiting the lease, and because it had been further advised that these instalments could also be recovered, if the claimant were successful at trial. That was incorrect advice, because paying money which you know is not due is not a mistake.

And yet, in relying on that wrong advice, the claimant paid the later instalments mistakenly thinking they were recoverable. So the court held that that mistake rendered the payments recoverable. But that meant that the wrong advice was right after all, meaning payment was not made under any mistake, in a Catch 22.

The better approach is as follows. The law of unjust enrichment should decide whether or not money is recoverable. If the law of unjust enrichment says money is not recoverable, then I should not be able to circumvent that law by claiming that I mistakenly thought the law of unjust enrichment said something else. Otherwise the law of unjust enrichment becomes whatever I mistakenly think it is. So a distinction should be drawn between making a mistake as to the law in general (which can be actionable), and making a mistake as to the law of unjust enrichment (which should not be actionable *in unjust enrichment*).

If, in *Nurdin & Peacock*, the landlord gets to retain the extra 5 instalments, paid by the tenant despite knowing them not to be due, that result is

49

entirely consistent with the cases which say that risky or doubtful payments cannot be recovered in unjust enrichment.

The law of unjust enrichment is not there to protect claimants from ill-advised behaviour. The law only intervenes when a higher threshold of injustice is crossed. The real unfairness in *Nurdin & Peacock* was that the tenant only paid the extra 5 instalments upon the advice of its lawyers. But that has nothing to do with the landlord. The tenant might instead sue the lawyers for negligent advice.

CHAPTER 5: DURESS

Unlawful act duress

5.1 Unlawful act duress is actionable in unjust enrichment.

5.2 This is where an accused makes a demand of the claimant, otherwise threatening to commit an unlawful act if the claimant does not comply.

5.3 The threat must coerce the claimant, and cause the resulting transaction.

Duress polices coercion.[64] Coercion is wrong to the extent that it forces a claimant to change their behaviour for the selfish reasons of the accused. This denies the claimant the freedom or autonomy to choose their own goals. It also denies them the dignity of an equal status, because it fails to respect them as having the capacity to choose such goals. And it deprives them of the chance to use or develop that capacity, when doing so can entail personal fulfilment and even social utility.

Not all coercion should be legally actionable. Like it or not, we are all of us sought to be persuaded, by subtle or strong-arm tactics, to behave contrary to how we might otherwise have chosen, by teachers or politicians or corporations or doctors and so on. Sometimes we even come to be grateful.

---

[64] Tamblyn, *The Law of Duress and Necessity*, ch 1

Thus it should not be actionable – and indeed, it is not actionable – for a parent to withhold a child's pocket money for them not doing their homework, or a customer to boycott a retailer whose products are tested on animals or made in sweatshops. We still need something more. One bright line is where the accused threatens to do something unlawful. So, if someone does an unlawful act, consequences follow, like criminal or tortious liability. If someone threatens an unlawful act, and for the purpose of being coercive, then a plea of duress might arise.

To this extent, duress polices coercive activity, by drawing a line consistent with the rest of the law: it outlaws the leveraging of activities which other areas of the law have already proscribed.

So what types of threatened unlawful act support a plea of duress? Threats of personal injury to the claimant,[65] or to someone for whom the claimant reasonably feels responsible.[66] Also perhaps threats of humiliation,[67] or threats to self-esteem or moral integrity.[68] Further, threats to damage or detain the claimant's goods,[69] or to harm the claimant's economic interests.[70] More generally, we might say that duress responds to threats of crime or tort.

---

[65] *Barton v Armstrong* [1976] AC 104; *Antonio v Antonio* [2010] EWHC 1199 (QB)

[66] *Royal Boskalis Westminster NV v Mountain* [1997] 2 All ER 929 (employees); *Gulf Azov Shipping Co Ltd v Idisi* [2001] EWCA Civ 491 (crew). Both also involved duress to goods. In the Canadian case of *Saxon v Saxon* [1976] 4 WWR 300, threats were made against the claimant's children.

[67] '*R' v HM Attorney General* [2003] UKPC 22 (threat to return special forces soldier to unit)

[68] *Halpern v Halpern* [2006] EWHC 603 (Comm), [85], [87], on appeal at [2007] EWCA Civ 291 (threats contrary to claimant's religious convictions)

[69] *Astley v Reynolds* (1731) 2 Str 915, 93 ER 939; *Maskell v Horner* [1915] 3 KB 106

54

It also responds to threats to breach contract.[71] While there is some discussion about the possibility of a threat to breach contract being nevertheless legitimate in some circumstances, those circumstances have never been properly identified, and no case has held a threatened breach to be legitimate.

Bad faith on the part of the accused might make the complainant feel more coerced.[72] And bad faith in the form of malice might be relevant to lawful act duress (see below). But otherwise, despite hesitant discussion of its relevance in the case law,[73] bad faith has no confirmed role to play in contractual duress, and has not been pivotal in any case.

It is important to distinguish between duress, and tough bargaining. In particular, it should be remembered, especially with compromise agreements, that parties often act as adversaries not collaborators, meaning that agreements are

---

[70] *North Ocean Shipping Co Ltd v Hyundai Construct Co Ltd, The Atlantic Baron* [1979] QB 705 ('*The Atlantic Baron*') (threat to interfere with lucrative charter party); *Universe Tankships Inc of Monrovia v International Transport Workers Federation, The Universe Sentinel* [1983] 1 AC 366 (threat not to tow ship out of port, and so leave it idling)

[71] *The Atlantic Baron* [1979] QB 705; *B&S Contracts and Design Ltd v Victor Green Publications Ltd* [1984] ICR 419; *Atlas Express Ltd v Kafco (Importers and Distributors) Ltd* [1989] QB 833; *Kolmar Group AG v Traxpo Enterprises Pvt Ltd* [2010] EWHC 113 (Comm); *Progress Bulk Carriers Ltd v Tube City IMS LLC* [2012] EWHC 273 (Comm). See too the line of Australian authorities cited with approval in *Occidental Worldwide Investment Corp v Skibs A/S Avanti, The Siboen and Sibotre* [1976] 1 Lloyd's Rep 293 ('*The Siboen and Sibotre*'), and *The Atlantic Baron* [1979] QB 705.

[72] *Huyton SA v Peter Cremer GmbH & Co* [2004] EWHC 1625 (Comm)

[73] *The Siboen and Sibotre* [1976] 1 Lloyd's Rep 293; *Huyton SA v Peter Cremer GmbH & Co* [2004] EWHC 1625 (Comm); *DSND Subsea Ltd v PGS Offshore Technology AS* [2000] All ER (D) 1101, [131]

often attended by circumstances of pressure.[74] The difference between duress and commercial pressure can be investigated forensically by searching for such probative facts as:[75] whether the claimant protested; or took steps to undo the transaction; and whether there was an alternative course open to him, such as an adequate legal remedy.

Whether the claimant knew it had reasonable alternatives goes to the question of coercion (ie the credibility of alleging it felt coerced). Ordinarily, if one has other options rather than acceding to the demand, one is likely to feel less pressurized. But otherwise it should hardly be a defence for an accused to say that the claimant should not have submitted to threats which the accused intended the claimant to submit to.

Examples from the case law

- The defendant threatened to kill the claimant unless the claimant agreed to restructure their company. The claimant agreed. He also agreed partly out of commercial necessity. Duress was made out (the agreement was set aside).[76]

- Ship builders threatened to breach the contract unless the purchasers increased the purchase price by the same amount as the currency had

---

[74] *Zebra Industries (Orogenesis Nova) Ltd v Wah Tong Paper Products Group Ltd* [2015] HKEC 1807

[75] *The Siboen and Sibotre* [1976] 1 Lloyd's Rep 293; *Pau On v Lau Yiu Long* [1980] AC 614

[76] *Barton v Armstrong* [1976] AC 104

been devalued. The purchasers did this. Economic duress was made out: the purchasers had agreed a very profitable charter for the new ship with Shell (a major market player); defaulting on the charter would have been detrimental to their relationship with Shell; it would have exposed them to a liability to Shell of about US$8m; there was no possibility of placing a substitute order with another builder for delivery in time; a substitute would anyway have cost nearly US$30m more; the charter stipulated for a new vessel, and so the purchasers could not have hired in a substitute; given the buoyant freight market, a substitute would have cost more to hire than Shell had agreed to pay anyway; the purchasers sought an alternative legal remedy by offering to arbitrate the point with the ship builders, even promising to pay the additional amount sought by them into escrow pending the outcome, but this offer was rejected.[77] (But the purchasers delayed in raising their plea of duress to such an extent that they were taken to have affirmed the variation.)

- A haulier threatened to refuse to deliver a seller's goods to his customers unless the seller agreed to pay the haulier more freight than was contractually due. This the seller agreed. Economic duress was made out: the seller was a small company whose commercial survival was dependent on fulfilling a large order to supply a major retail chain; it would have been difficult if not impossible to find alternative hauliers,

---

[77] *The Atlantic Baron* [1979] QB 705

especially at that time of year (the run-up to Christmas); and non-delivery would have resulted in the retailer bringing proceedings against the seller and ceasing to trade with it. The haulier could not recover the additional freight.[78]

- An accused refused to complete an agreement to sell a building unless the complainant entered into a guarantee, which it did. That guarantee was later called upon. Duress was not made out. Rather, said the court, the claimant considered the matter thoroughly, chose to avoid litigation, and formed the opinion that the risk in giving the guarantee was more apparent than real.[79] In other words, the claimant agreed to the guarantee because it thought the demand of insufficient consequence. The claimant was not coerced. Although the accused's demand was the sole reason for providing the guarantee (it would not have been provided if the accused had not demanded it), that was not enough to sustain a plea of duress.

Lawful act duress

People should be able to make lawful threats. For example, it should be possible to threaten a boycott unless a producer stops animal testing, or while a nightclub bans black musicians.[80] Nevertheless, there is some discussion in the case law that a

---

[78] *Atlas Express Ltd v Kafco (Importers and Distributers) Ltd* [1989] QB 833

[79] *Pau On v Lau Yiu Long* [1980] AC 614

[80] *Scala Ballroom (Wolverhampton) Ltd v Ratcliffe* [1958] 3 All ER 220

threat to commit a lawful act might also support a plea of duress.[81] Now, given that the accused does not threaten anything unlawful, a different ingredient is needed to differentiate between forceful persuasion or protest, and illegitimate coercion.

The best candidate is where the accused threatens to inflict harm maliciously (albeit lawfully). To act this way, that is, simply to see another bend to one's will or otherwise suffer, is to treat them, not as a person, but as an object of sport, or a tool for self-gratification. To do this, and then hide behind one's legal rights, is a cynical misuse of rights. Instead of using rights to guard one's freedoms or advance one's own ends, they become instead the means of subordinating and dominating others. This is an abuse of rights, and the law need not tolerate it.

Having said all this, no case has been decided on the basis of lawful act duress. Further, there is no pressing need to recognise the notion of lawful act duress after all. There is already the doctrine of unconscionable conduct which renders illegitimate the exploitation of a victim through otherwise lawful means (see chapter 7).

Often bracketed together with lawful act duress is the idea of threatening a claimant with criminal prosecution or civil litigation if they do not comply with the demand:

However, genuine threats of criminal prosecution are best understood as a distinctive category. They will usually include, in return for complying with the

---

[81] *CTN Cash and Carry Ltd v Gallaher Ltd* [1994] 4 All ER 714

demand, an agreement not to prosecute, and that is invalid anyway as a matter of public policy.[82]

Otherwise, threats of criminal prosecution or civil litigation should only constitute duress if what is threatened amounts to the torts of malicious prosecution, or abuse of process – in other words, if what is threatened is otherwise unlawful (because tortious) after all.

The tort of malicious prosecution requires prosecution without reasonable and probable cause, and from malice. Malice here means spite, or an improper motive such as using the process of the court for an ulterior benefit other than bringing a person to justice.[83] (It also applies to civil proceedings.)[84] Similarly, the tort of abuse of process applies to those proceedings, even if well founded, whose purpose is not the vindication of the claimant's rights in those proceedings, but some ulterior purpose outside the ambit of the claim, so that the suit is used as an instrument of extortion in an unconnected matter.[85] (All of which again sounds like an abuse of rights.)

Beyond that, threats of civil litigation should be resisted. It makes little sense, for example, to buckle before a threat of civil litigation, and pay the accused, only to bring civil litigation in order to recover that payment.

[82] *Williams v Bayley* (1866) LR 1 HL 200. Money paid over was recovered in *Davies v London and Provincial Marine Insurance Co* (1878) 8 Ch D 469. The most appropriate unjust factor might now be failure of basis.

[83] *Gibbs v Rea* [1998] AC 786, 797; *Williamson v Attorney General of Trinidad and Tobago* [2014] UKPC 29, [12]

[84] *Willers v Joyce (No 1)* [2016] UKSC 43

[85] *Speed Seal Products Ltd v Paddington* [1986] 1 All ER 91

Third parties

A recipient may be liable in unjust enrichment if he applied the duress himself, or had actual knowledge that the transaction was procured by another's duress. Constructive knowledge (what a reasonable person might have known) seems less appropriate. If, central to the moral wrong of coercion, is the accused's manipulation of the claimant to his own ends, then a party seemingly has done nothing wrong who neither has effected that manipulation nor takes the benefit of another's known manipulation. (But constructive knowledge may be relevant in property law – see chapter 6.)

CHAPTER 6: UNDUE INFLUENCE

Nature of undue influence

6.1 Undue influence is actionable in unjust enrichment. It involves leveraging a relationship of influence in order to procure a transaction.

In broad terms, undue influence is where a relationship gives one party ascendancy or influence over another, and he exploits or abuses that influence in order to procure a transaction.[86] To this extent, there may be considerable overlap with a plea of unconscionable conduct (see chapter 7). As for why we recognise undue influence, Chen-Wishart's explanation seems attractive, that this is all about protecting and vindicating important social relationships of trust and confidence.[87]

From the case law, a common theme emerges on how undue influence is characterised. Thus, a claimant 'may be led but must not be driven and her will must be the offspring of her own volition, not a record of someone else's.'[88] There must not be 'complete domination by [the accused] over [the claimant] so that the mind of the latter became a mere channel through which the wishes of the former flowed'.[89] The situation to avoid is where 'the pen may have been the pen of [the

---

[86] *Tate v Williamson* (1866) 2 Ch App 55, 61; *Royal Bank of Scotland plc v Etridge (No 2)* [2001] UKHL 44, [6]; *National Commercial Bank (Jamaica) Ltd v Hew* [2003] UKPC 51, [29]-[31], [34]; *'R' v Attorney-General for England and Wales* [2003] UKPC 22, [21]

[87] Chen-Wishart 2006

[88] *Drew v Daniel* [2005] EWCA Civ 507, [36]

claimant], the mind was the mind of [the accused]'.[90] Or where there has been such domination that the complainant 'acts as the mere puppet of the dominator'.[91]

6.2 Undue influence can be proven in two ways: as actual undue influence, or presumed undue influence.

It is sometimes said that there are two 'types' of undue influence, actual and presumed, although really these are just two different ways of proving undue influence. With presumed undue influence, the claimant proves undue influence by using an evidential presumption which the defendant fails to rebut. With actual undue influence, the claimant proves undue influence without relying upon an evidential presumption. (Sometimes actual undue influence is called 'class 1' undue influence, while presumed undue influence is called 'class 2'.)

Once it is shown that the transaction was procured by undue influence, there is no need for the claimant to go further and show that he would not otherwise have entered into the transaction.[92]

---

[89] *Tufton v Sperni* [1952] 2 TLR 516, 519, 532

[90] *Dunbar Bank plc v Nadeem* [1998] 3 All ER 876, 883

[91] *Lloyd's Bank Ltd v Bundy* [1975] QB 326, 342

[92] *UCB Corporate Services Ltd v Williams* [2002] EWCA Civ 555

Actual undue influence

6.3 Actual undue influence involves: (i) improper acts by the accused, overt and proven; (ii) which influenced the claimant; and (iii) which caused the transaction.

The claimant must show that the accused had the capacity to influence him, did influence him, unduly, and that this caused the transaction.[93] To the extent that actual undue influence consists of overt acts of improper pressure or coercion, then there is also an overlap with duress (see chapter 5).[94] It is not a necessary legal ingredient of actual undue influence that the claimant proves the transaction to be to his manifest disadvantage,[95] but it is a usual factual indicator that influence has been unduly exercised.[96]

Examples from the case law

- When an elderly man, enfeebled mentally and physically, was admitted to hospital, the defendant threatened not to let him return home to his

---

[93] *Bank of Credit and Commerce International SA v Aboody* [1990] 1 QB 923, 967 (CA); *CP Motors Ltd v On Chit Transportation Ltd* [2014] HKCU 1004, [73]; *Chow Ki Chuen v Choi Lin Fung Ada* [2014] HKCU 291, [25]

[94] *Royal Bank of Scotland plc v Etridge (No 2)* [2001] UKHL 44, [8]

[95] *CIBC Mortgages plc v Pitt* [1994] 1 AC 200

[96] *Royal Bank of Scotland plc v Etridge (No 2)* [2001] UKHL 44, [12]

lodgings of 40 years unless he cut off all contact with his family, and changed his will in favour of the defendant. That will was set aside.[97]

- A nephew coerced his aging aunt to sign a deed, conferring on him a significant benefit to the detriment of her own son, after a lengthy and distressing conversation which included a threat to sue her, matters which he concealed from the son. The deed was set aside.[98]

- After his wife died, the elderly claimant was befriended by a younger defendant, who extracted £1.9m of gifts over 15 years, latterly by methods culminating in verbal onslaughts and physical violence. Those later payments were recovered.[99]

- The non-disclosure by the husband of his affair (eventually leading to divorce) was an abuse of the trust and confidence placed in him by his wife, which otherwise led to an obligation of fairness and candour. So when she agreed to charge their house to cover his credit card debts, not knowing of the affair, the mortgage could be set aside for undue influence.[100]

[97] *Killick v Pountney* [1999] All ER (D) 365; see too *Langton v Langton* [1995] 3 FCR 521

[98] *Drew v Daniel* [2005] EWCA Civ 507

[99] *Clarke v Prus* [1995] NPC 41

[100] *Hewett v First Plus Financial Group plc* [2010] 2 P&CR 22; *Yang Foo-Oi v Wai Wai Chen* [2016]

Presumed undue influence

6.4 To raise a rebuttable presumption of undue influence, the claimant must show: (i) a relationship of trust and confidence between the parties; and (ii) that the transaction calls for an explanation, or is not readily explicable on ordinary motives.

To raise a rebuttable presumption of undue influence, the claimant must show that he placed trust and confidence in the accused in the management of his financial affairs, along with a transaction which calls for explanation.[101] At which point, it is rebuttably presumed that the reason for the claimant's transaction was the accused's undue influence.

As for (i):

In certain categories, a relationship of trust and confidence is assumed automatically and cannot be challenged, for example: parent and child, trustee and beneficiary, solicitor and client, doctor and patient.[102] (Sometimes this is called 'class 2A' undue influence.) Otherwise, a relationship of trust and confidence must be proven on the facts, and this has happened in such relationships as: husband and wife;[103] adult son and elderly parents;[104] elderly man and his secretary / companion;[105]

HKCU 2874 (CFI)

[101] *Royal Bank of Scotland plc v Etridge (No 2)* [2001] UKHL 44, [14]

[102] *Royal Bank of Scotland plc v Etridge (No 2)* [2001] UKHL 44, [18]

[103] *Royal Bank of Scotland plc v Etridge (No 2)* [2001] UKHL 44

[104] *Avon Finance Co Ltd v Bridger* [1985] 2 All ER 281

customer and his bank;[106] pop singer and his or her manager;[107] a junior employee and her employer;[108] soldier and his commanding office.[109] (Sometimes this is called 'class 2B'.)

As for (ii):

The transaction must call for an explanation, or be not readily explicable by the relationship of the parties,[110] or not reasonably accounted for on the ground of friendship, relationship, charity, or other ordinary motives on which ordinary people act.[111] The greater the disadvantage to the vulnerable party, the more cogent must be the explanation.[112]

Examples of transactions which call for an explanation include: giving away such property that the claimant might be unable to provide for herself or himself in the future,[113] or only precariously;[114] or giving away property so that the claimant might not be able to provide for other loved ones or cherished interests,[115]

[105] *Re Craig* [1971] Ch 95

[106] *Lloyd's Bank Ltd v Bundy* [1975] QB 326; *National Commercial Bank (Jamaica) Ltd v Hew* [2003] UKPC 51

[107] *O'Sullivan v Management Agency and Music Ltd* [1985] QB 428; *Kwok Wing Kiu v Boxing Promotions Ltd* [2013] HKCU 1191

[108] *Credit Lyonnais Bank Nederland NV v Burch* [1997] 1 All ER 144

[109] *'R' v Attorney-General for England and Wales* [2003] UKPC 22

[110] *Royal Bank of Scotland plc v Etridge (No 2)* [2001] UKHL 44, [21]-[29]

[111] *Allcard v Skinner* (1887) 36 Ch D 145, 185

[112] *Royal Bank of Scotland plc v Etridge (No 2)* [2001] UKHL 44, [24]

[113] *Allcard v Skinner* (1887) 36 Ch D 145; *Hammond v Osborn* [2002] EWCA Civ 885; *Hart v Burbidge* [2014] EWCA Civ 992

[114] *Cheese v Thomas* [1994] 1 All ER 35

with the transaction instead being very much to the financial advantage of the defendant.[116]

For example, the deceased sold her house and paid the proceeds to her daughter. The court held that there had been a relationship of trust and confidence, in which the defendant had been in the ascendancy and the deceased had been vulnerable. The nature, size and effect of the gift was such that it was out of the ordinary and called for an explanation: it effectively deprived the beneficiaries under her will of all their inheritance, and it left the deceased, while alive, with little money to fund her future life, including her care home and nursing fees. The court ordered the gift to be repaid to the deceased's estate.[117]

---

[115] *Randall v Randall* [2004] EWHC 2258 (Ch); *Pesticcio v Huet* [2004] EWCA Civ 372

[116] *Pearce v Beverley* [2013] EWHC 2627 (Ch)

[117] *Re Estate of Joyce Smith (Deceased); Kicks v Leigh* [2014] EWHC 3926 (Ch)

Rebutting the presumption

6.5 Presumed undue influence can be rebutted by the defendant giving an adequate explanation of the transaction, or showing it to be the result of the claimant's full, free and informed consent.

Thus improvident mortgages by parents to support loans to their children are capable of explanation on the basis of ordinary parental affection.[118] Similarly, there is no requirement for a bank to save its customer from taking out an improvident loan.[119]

In one case, a special forces soldier had signed a confidentiality agreement at the request of his commanding officer and against a threat of otherwise being required to leave the special forces. He wished to set it aside and write his memoirs. The court said that, while there was a relationship of influence between a special forces soldier and his commanding officer, the confidentiality agreement the soldier was asked to sign was one which anyone who wished to continue serving in the special forces could reasonably have been required to sign, to maintain security of operations and personnel.[120]

---

[118] *Portman Building Society v Dusangh* [2000] 2 All ER (Comm) 221 (where the claimant unsuccessfully pleaded unconscionable conduct); *Yien Yieh Commercial Bank Ltd v Hung Oi Wah* [2009] HKCU 1668, upheld on appeal [2011] HKCU 633

[119] *National Commercial Bank (Jamaica) Ltd v Hew* [2003] UKPC 51

[120] *'R' v Attorney-General for England and Wales* [2003] UKPC 22

In another case, where a farm was partitioned, the defendant's larger share merely reflected the fact that she had contributed the majority of the original purchase price, and provided the main financial support for the farming business.[121] And where a father transferred most of his assets as a gift to his son and daughter-in-law, without providing for his other two children, this reflected the care which the father had received over many years from the donees, in contrast to his estrangement from the other children on account of their alienating behaviour.[122]

Alternatively, the defendant might need to show that the transaction was the result of the claimant's free will,[123] or full, free and informed consent,[124] usually by showing that the claimant had independent advice. That advice must be competent and honest, and given in full knowledge of all the relevant circumstances.[125] But just because the claimant had advice, or even understood the full implications of the transaction, it does not follow that he was free of influence.[126] And in some cases, a transaction is so wholly improvident that no competent solicitor could advise in its favour.[127] But where the claimant has given informed

---

[121] *Liddle v Cree* [2011] EWHC 3294 (Ch); see too *Brown v Stephenson* [2013] EWHC 2531 (Ch)

[122] *Bateman v Overy* [2014] EWHC 432 (Ch)

[123] *Allcard v Skinner* (1887) 36 Ch the defendant 145, 171

[124] *Zamet v Hyman* [1961] 3 All ER 933, 1446; *Goodchild v Bradbury* [2006] All ER (D) 247 (Dec)

[125] *Inche Noriah v Shaik Allie bin Omar* [1929] AC 127

[126] *Royal Bank of Scotland plc v Etridge (No 2)* [2001] UKHL 44, [20]; *Davies v AIB Group (UK) plc* [2012] EWHC 2178 (Ch); *Farshneshani v Zaiwalla* [2014] EWHC 3294 (Ch); *Re Estate of Joyce Smith (Deceased); Kicks v Leigh* [2014] EWHC 3926 (Ch)

[127] *Credit Lyonnais Bank Nederland NV v Burch* [1997] 1 All ER 144, 156-157

consent, that is the end of the matter, however improvident the transaction might appear.[128]

Third parties

A recipient may be liable in unjust enrichment if he exercised undue influence himself, or had actual knowledge that the transaction was procured by another's undue influence.

For example, adult daughter A unduly influenced aging mother B to make generous gifts shortly before the mother's death, to the detriment of the beneficiaries under B's will. This also tainted A's husband C, who knew of the influence, and who benefitted from the gifts. C could be sued for his enrichment.[129]

Constructive knowledge (what a reasonable person might have known) can be relevant in property law.[130] For example, one person may have a legal interest in property, but another person has an equitable interest. Which takes priority? The law has decided that the legal interest takes priority, unless the legal owner had actual or contrastive knowledge of the equitable interest.

The most common situation is where a husband exerts undue influence over his wife in order to procure a mortgage of their home to the bank. The bank thereby gets a legal interest in the property. But this cannot be enforced against the wife if the bank had actual or constructive knowledge of the undue influence.[131]

---

[128] *Bank of China (Hong Kong) Ltd v Wong Kong Sing* [2002] 1 HKLRD 358

[129] *Hart v Burbidge* [2013] EWHC 1628 (Ch), affirmed [2014] EWCA Civ 992

[130] See also chapter 7 (unconscionable conduct)

(The best explanation seems to be that the undue influence creates the equitable proprietary interest – see also chapter 16.)

This principle is not limited to husband and wife relationships. Any lender is 'put on inquiry' whenever the relationship between surety and debtor is non-commercial.[132] Thus a plea of undue influence was also available where a junior employee put up her flat as security for her employer.[133]

If a bank, which has no actual knowledge of any undue influence, also wants to be free of any constructive knowledge, then it must take reasonable steps to ensure that the wife is properly advised, and gave her consent with independence. (The precise steps a bank must take are detailed in the case law.)[134]

Otherwise, outside of property law, constructive knowledge seems less appropriate to unjust enrichment. If abuse of a relationship of trust is central to the moral wrong of undue influence, then a party has seemingly done nothing wrong who neither commits that abuse nor take's knowing advantage of another's abuse.

---

[131] *Royal Bank of Scotland plc v Etridge (No 2)* [2001] UKHL 44

[132] *Royal Bank of Scotland plc v Etridge (No 2)* [2001] UKHL 44, [87]

[133] *Credit Lyonnais Bank Nederland NV v Burch* [1997] 1 All ER 144

[134] *Royal Bank of Scotland plc v Etridge (No 2)* [2001] UKHL 44

CHAPTER 7: UNCONSCIONABLE CONDUCT

Defining unconscionable conduct

7.1 Unconscionable conduct is actionable in unjust enrichment.

7.2 It is where the claimant suffers a special weakness, which the accused exploits in order to procure the transaction.

7.3 The transaction is then impugned unless the accused shows it to be fair and reasonable.

The doctrine of unconscionable conduct seeks to uphold the dignity of the complainant as an end in themselves, rather than having them treated as an object for exploitation, or merely a means to a quick profit.[135]

The complainant must suffer a special weakness.[136] In general terms, this is when the complainant is unable to judge or advance their best interests.[137] But the special weakness must go beyond the personal or idiosyncratic urges and

---

[135] Tamblyn, *The Law of Duress and Necessity*, ch 2

[136] *Earl of Chesterfield v Jansen* (1750) 2 Ves Sen 125; 28 ER 82; *Earl of Aylesford v Morris* (1873) LR 8 Ch App 484; *Fry v Lane* (1888) 40 Ch D 312; *Alec Lobb (Garages) Ltd v Total Oil GB Ltd;* [1983] 1 All ER 944, upheld on appeal [1985] 1 All ER 303

[137] *Commercial Bank of Australia Ltd v Amadio* (1983) 57 ALJR 358; *Australian Competition and Consumer Commission v C G Berbatis Holdings Pty Ltd* (2003) 77 AJLR 926

predilections which everyday lead us to transact. Thus a gambler who chooses to gamble is not necessarily exploited by a casino who lawfully provides him with the opportunity to satiate his desire.[138] Special weakness is judged relative to the accused,[139] because the ability of the accused to take advantage of the weakness is of central importance. A wide range of relevant weakness is acknowledged, including ignorance, basic need, and diminished mental capacity or fortitude.[140]

The accused must exploit the claimant's weakness.[141] Note that exploitation can be active, or it can be passive acceptance of a benefit in unconscionable circumstances.[142] Behaviour which is unconscionable or exploitative is abhorrent to current standards of social morality. It is not a marginal case of misbehaviour. Rather, it 'shocks the conscience of the court'.[143]

The terms of the transaction do not need to be unfair in themselves; simply procuring the transaction might be unconscionable.[144] But substantive unfairness is strong evidence from which weakness and exploitation can be

---

[138] *Kakavas v Crown Melbourne Ltd* (2013) 87 ALJR 708

[139] *Earl of Aylesford v Morris* (1873) LR 8 Ch App 484; *Alec Lobb (Garages) Ltd v Total Oil GB Ltd* [1983] 1 All ER 944, upheld on appeal [1985] 1 All ER 303; *Jones v Morgan* [2002] 1 EGLR 125

[140] *Blomley v Ryan* (1956) 99 CLR 362

[141] *Hart v O'Connor* [1985] AC 1000

[142] *Hart v O'Connor* [1985] AC 1000; *Louth v Diprose* (1992) 67 ALJR 95; *Nichols v Jessup* [1986] 1 NZLR 226

[143] *Alec Lobb (Garages) Ltd v Total Oil GB Ltd* [1983] 1 All ER 944, upheld on appeal [1985] 1 All ER 303

[144] *Commercial Bank of Australia Ltd v Amadio* (1983) 57 ALJR 358; *Standard Chartered Bank v Shem Yin Fun* [2002] HKEC 582

inferred. Further, the more unfair the contract, the less credible any assertion by the accused that he did not perceive or exploit any weakness.

Upon proof of the above, unconscionable bargain is presumptively made out. The accused then bears the burden of showing the transaction to be fair and reasonable.[145]

Proper legal advice can enable an accused to judge and advance its best interests after all. In other words, it can compensate for, and so eliminate, many relative weaknesses. But advice on its own cannot obviate a basic need or state of necessity. Also, independent advice does not make a transaction fair and reasonable, if the advice is ignored,[146] or is advice which no competent lawyer could proffer.[147]

Examples from the case law

- A young expectant heir took out a loan at an extortionate rate of interest to pay off his debts. There was weakness on one side (unprotected youth, inexperience, and 'moral imbecility'), and extortion or unconscientious advantage taken on the other (by charging 60% interest). The defendant failed to show that the transaction was fair, just and reasonable. The claimant was held liable to repay the principal plus interest of only 5%.[148]

---

[145] *Earl of Aylesford v Morris* (1873) LR 8 Ch App 484

[146] *Boustany v Pigott* (1993) 42 WIR 175

[147] *Fry v Lane* (1888) 40 Ch D 312; *Credit Lyonnais Bank Nederland NV v Burch* [1997] 1 All ER 144; *Portman Building Society v Dusangh* [2000] All ER (D) 582; *Jones v Morgan* [2002] 1 EGLR 125

- A lease was set aside when the defendant took advantage of the nephew's absence to renegotiate favourable terms with the claimant, who was old and confused, and whose affairs were usually managed by the nephew. This was despite the fact that the claimant was advised by her solicitor against the transaction.[149]

- There was *no* unconscionable bargain where the defendant, elderly, illiterate, speaking little English, and on a low income, took out a mortgage to give money to his son to open a supermarket, which failed. The transaction was improvident, but there was no exploitation by the building society, who did not act in a morally reprehensible manner, and whose duty was not to police transactions to ensure that parents were wise in seeking to assist their children.[150]

- A contract for the sale of farmland was *not* set aside even though the farmer selling it was suffering from mental incapacity. The purchaser did not know, let alone to take advantage of it, and the vendor was independently advised.[151]

---

[148] *Aylesford v Morris* (1873) LR 8 Ch App 484

[149] *Boustany v Pigott* (1993) 69 P&CR 298

[150] *Portman Building Society v Dusangh* [2000] 2 All ER (Comm) 221

[151] *Hart v O'Connor* [1985] AC 1000

Third parties

A recipient may be liable in unjust enrichment if he behaved unconscionably, or had actual knowledge (or willful blindness) that the transaction was procured by another's unconscionable conduct. But liability should not follow for knowledge which the recipient reasonably should have known, but did not know.[152] As Bigwood says, an accused cannot exploit someone's weakness if he should have known, but did not in fact know, of that weakness.[153] But to repeat, the more outrageous the transaction, the less credible is any denial that he neither noticed nor exploited any weakness. (But constructive knowledge, ie what a reasonable person might have known, is relevant in property law – see chapter 6.)

---

[152] *Kakavas v Crown Melbourne Ltd* (2013) 87 ALJR 708

[153] Bigwood 2005: 71

CHAPTER 8: FAILURE OF BASIS

When restitution available

Here is an example of this unjust factor. The claimant pays £100 to the defendant for apples. The defendant does not supply the apples. The claimant may be able to recover his payment. The injustice is the defendant keeping the money when the claimant does not get the performance he expected, this being the basis on which he gave the money in the first place.

This unjust factor is traditionally called 'total failure of consideration'. The language of 'consideration' derives from the pre-history of unjust enrichment as 'quasi-contract' (see chapter 1). But unjust enrichment is now an independent cause of action. The claimant can also seek restitution under this head in non-contractual settings, as we shall see. And even in contractual settings, it is not necessarily the failure of contractual consideration, technically construed as the counter-*promise*, which matters, so much as the actual *carrying out* of that promise.[154]

Virgo calls it 'failure of basis'.[155] So too do the editors of *Goff & Jones*,[156] and it seems to be gaining traction with the court.[157] Virgo then defines 'basis' as

---

[154] *Fibrosa Spolka Akcyjna v Fairbairn Lawson Combe Barbour Ltd* [1943] AC 32, 48; *Roxborough v Rothmans of Pall Mall Ltd* (2001) 208 CLR 516, [16]

[155] Virgo 2015: ch 13

[156] Mitchel et al 2016: ch 12

[157] *Barnes v Eastenders Cash & Carry plc* [2014] UKSC 26, [105]-[106]

the condition pursuant to which a transaction occurred. If that condition is not satisfied, there is a failure of basis. But that would seem wide enough to cover mistake as well. So he further explains that failure of basis is not an unjust factor itself, but rather a general principle underlying three situations. First, where the claimant does not get the performance which he expected from the defendant. Second, where a contract is frustrated. But the financial consequences here are governed by a statutory scheme which is as much about sharing loss as it is restitution.[158] Third, where a transaction is void.

So we must understand that 'failure of basis' has a specific and technical meaning. It can be summarised as follows:

8.1 The claimant can seek restitution when he fails to receive what he legitimately expected of the transaction.

Note that the performance must be *legitimately* expected. It cannot amount to mere wishful thinking, or risk or mis-prediction, something not usually sufficient to support a claim in unjust enrichment (see chapter 4.2).[159] Otherwise, restitution may be available in a diverse range of circumstances:

---

[158] Law Reform (Frustrated Contracts) Act 1943; *Gamerco SA v ICM / Fair Warning (Agency) Ltd* [1995] 1 WLR 1226

[159] Virgo 2015: 309-310 says that the basis must be communicated between the claimant and defendant, giving the defendant an opportunity to object, such that the basis can be considered a shared understanding between the parties.

I. Where the claimant can escape a bad bargain. For example, the claimant bought shares from the defendant, but the defendant failed to transfer the shares into the claimant's name. The claimant terminated the contract for repudiatory breach. The claimant recovered the purchase price, despite the fact that the shares had fallen in value.[160]

II. Where the claimant can recover more than the original contract price. For example, where the defendant prevented the claimant from completing its construction work, the claimant was entitled to treat the contract as at an end and claim the value of its work so far, even above the contract price.[161]

III. Where the claimant is the contract-breaker. For example, the claimant part paid in advance, but then failed, in breach of contract, to pay the balance or take delivery. The defendant elected to treat the contract as at an end. The claimant could recover his payment (subject to any counterclaim by the defendant).[162]

---

[160] *Wilkinson v Lloyd* (1845) 7 QB 27

[161] *Lodder v Slowey* [1904] AC 442; see too *Rover International Ltd v Cannon Film Sales Ltd (No 3)* [1989] 3 All ER 423; but in contrast, see *Taylor v Motability Finance Ltd* [2004] EWHC 2619, *Elek v Bar-Tur* [2013] EWHC 207 (Ch). See chapter 2.2 above.

[162] *Dies v British and International Mining and Finance Corporation Ltd* [1939] 1 KB 724; see too *Korea Building Materials Trading Corp v Hong Kong Dongil Trading Co Ltd* [1993] 2 HKC 423. In *Thomas v Brown* (1876) 1 QBD 714, 723, it was said that, where the defendant remains ready, willing and able to perform, the claimant cannot recover any advance payment. Perhaps it matters that in *Dies*, the defendant had accepted the claimant's repudiatory breach, and so terminated the contract, whereas in *Thomas v Brown*, the defendant might be taken as not having accepted the claimant's repudiatory

IV. Where a promise is not contractually enforceable. For example, the claimant agreed orally with his aunt to do various services for her in return for her leaving him a house in her will. She did not leave him the house. The claimant could not claim the house (ie he could not enforce an oral contract for property), so instead he could recover the value of his services from the estate.[163]

Similarly, the claimant incurred expense obtaining planning permission for the defendant's property, on the defendant's promise that thereafter the claimant could buy the property and develop it and share the profits with the defendant. That promise was unenforceable because it failed to comply with statutory formalities. But when the defendant reneged on the promise anyway, the claimant could recover the value of its services.[164]

However, in some circumstances, the policy which renders a contract unenforceable for failure to comply with statutory formalities also precludes circumventing that by a claim in unjust enrichment. Put another way, there is no legitimate expectation of any performance which is contrary to statute.

So where a person hired a car pursuant to a regulated consumer credit agreement which was unenforceable for non-compliance with statutory formalities,

---

breach, thus keeping the contract alive. But *Thomas v Brown* is probably just bad law. It is inconsistent, for example, with the modern law which says that advance payments on account of what is due under a contract are recoverable by the payer if the contract is not completed, even if that is due to the fault of the payer, subject to the payee setting off his claim for damages: *Polyset Ltd v Panhandat Ltd* (2002) 5 HKCFAR 234. That modern law is instead consistent with *Dies.*

[163] *Deglman v Guaranty Trust Co of Canada* [1954] 3 DLR 785

[164] *Yeoman's Row Management Ltd v Cobbe* [2008] UKHL 55; see too *Singh v Sanghera* [2013] EWHC 956 (Ch)

no hire was payable in contract. Nor could this result be circumvented, by suing in unjust enrichment for the use of the car, because that would otherwise undermine the purpose of the statutory regime.[165] Similarly, a loan which was unenforceable because it failed to comply with statutory formalities could not be recovered in unjust enrichment either.[166]

V. Where a promised contract never materializes. For example, a claimant submitted a tender to carry out building works to premises which had suffered war damage. The defendant led the claimant to believe that the contract would be awarded to the claimant and requested a more detailed estimate (ie the claimant had a legitimate expectation of being remunerated for this detailed estimate). The defendant then used that detailed estimate to make its own claim to the War Damage Commission, and sold the land without doing the work. The claimant could recover the value of its work done on the detailed estimate.[167]

Similarly, the claimant could claim the value of steel manufactured and delivered (and used by the defendant) in anticipation of a contract which then never materialized because the parties could not ultimately agree all the terms.[168]

In contrast, the claimant submitted a tender which the defendant accepted 'subject to contract'. When negotiations fell through because ultimately the site

---

[165] *Dimond v Lovell* [2002] 1 AC 384, 397-398

[166] *Barons Finance Ltd v Makanju* [2013] EWHC 153 (Ch)

[167] *William Lacey (Hounslow) Ltd v Davis* [1957] 2 All ER 712; see too *Countrywide Communications Ltd v ICL Pathway* [1999] All ER (D) 1192

[168] *British Steel Corpn v Cleveland Bridge and Engineering Co Ltd* [1984] 1 All ER 504

could not be developed, the claimant sought restitution for its efforts, but was denied. Both parties knew these were negotiations from which either could walk away freely. In other words, performance was not legitimately expected – the claimant was a risk-taker. (And since the site could not be developed, the defendant had not benefitted from the claimant's preparatory work.)[169]

VI. Where a transaction is void. For example, banks entered into interest rate swap agreements with local authorities. It was subsequently ruled that the local authorities were acting ultra vires, rendering the contracts void. For this reason alone it was considered that payments might be recovered.[170] The point seems to be that the parties expected to get legally enforceable rights, and this expectation was disappointed. Similarly, a claimant who bought a car, and used it, only later to discover that the car was stolen, so that he got no legal rights as owner, was able to recover the purchase price.[171] An easier route might now be to plead mistake of law.

---

[169] *Regalian Properties Ltd v London Docklands Development Corpn* [1995] 1 All ER 1005

[170] *Westdeutsche Landesbank Girozentrale v Islington LBC* [1994] 4 All ER 890, on appeal [1996] AC 669; *Guinness Mahon & Co Ltd v Kensington and Chelsea Royal LBC* [1999] QB 215; *Haugesund Kommune v Depfa SCA Bank* [2010] EWCA Civ 579

[171] *Rowland v Divall* [1923] 2 KB 500; *Butterworth v Kingsway Motors Ltd* [1954] 2 All ER 694; *Barber v NWS Bank plc* [1996] 1 All ER 906. But where a buyer did get title, and used the car, only the car turned out to be of worse quality than expected, the bargain was not a total failure: *Yeoman Credit Ltd v Apps* [1962] 2 QB 508

Whether failure must be total

Traditionally, the claimant must get nothing at all of what he expected in return. 'There can be no unjust enrichment where payments are made pursuant to a valid contract which is fully *or partly* performed'.[172]

<u>Examples from the case law</u>

- A ship sank 8 days into a fortnight cruise. There was no restitution because the cruise had not been a total failure.[173]

- A master watchmaker died after one year into a 6 year apprenticeship. There was no restitution of the advance payment.[174]

- The parties entered into a contract for the design, build and sale of a ship, to be paid for in instalments. When the seller sued for an instalment, the buyer could not claim that there had been a total failure of expectation. Although the buyer had no ship to use, nevertheless it had received some of what it had bargained for, namely design and build.[175]

---

[172] *Madoff Securities International Ltd v Raven* [2013] EWHC 3147 (Comm), [376]

[173] *Baltic Shipping Co v Dillon, The Mikhail Lermontov* (1993) 176 CLR 344

[174] *Whincup v Hughes* (1871) LR 6 CP 78

[175] *Stocznia Gdanska SA v Latvian Shipping Co* [1998] 1 All ER 883

However, some cases indicate that, if a contract is severable, or if payment might somehow be apportioned to different aspects of performance, then some of the payment can be recovered, if the corresponding aspect of performance totally failed.[176]

Some cases stretch this analysis to breaking point – which thus suggests that *partial* failure of expectation might suffice.

For example, in repudiatory breach of contract, builders left site having been paid £26k for work worth £22k. It was held that £4k was recoverable, that part having been paid for no performance.[177]

In another case, a loan had been given under a mortgage subsequently avoided. The lender could recover the capital sum of the loan. This was so, even though two interest payments had been made. At least it might be possible to view capital and interest as severable. But the court went further, and expressed a willingness to have allowed recovery even if some capital repayments had been made.[178]

The most that can be said is this. Traditionally, there must be a total failure of expectation. But if a contract can be severed or apportioned, there might be total failure of a part, and restitution in respect of that part is recoverable. There is, moreover, a movement perhaps towards recognising partial failure of

---

[176] *Guido Van Der Garde BV v Force India Formula One Team Ltd* [2010] EWHC 2373 (QB); *Barnes v Eastenders Cash & Carry plc* [2014] UKSC 26, [114]. Statute might even provide for apportionment: Apportionment Act 1870; *Item Software (UK) Ltd v Fassihi* [2004] EWCA Civ 1244

[177] *DO Ferguson & Associates v Sohl* (1992) Times, 24 December; 62 BLR 95

[178] *Goss v Chilcott* [1996] AC 788, 798

expectation. That does not seem objectionable. After all, the defendant too is well protected through the defence of change of position (see chapter 11), and the possibility of bringing a counterclaim for restitution in respect of any benefit which the claimant has received in turn (see chapter 13).

CHAPTER 9: LEGAL COMPULSION

9.1 Where the claimant is compelled, by legal process, to pay a third party, thereby also discharging the defendant's legal liability to that third party, the claimant can seek restitution from the defendant.

At one level, of course, there is no injustice: the claimant was himself legally obliged to pay. But at another level, the complaint seems to be that the defendant's liability had priority, or that the defendant should at least pay his share.

Ultimately, this is all about policy: it is thought proper that the third party is ensured a full remedy, thus the third party can proceed against anyone to blame, the claimant or the defendant. Afterwards, the law fine-tunes the shares between the claimant and the defendant.

So if a claimant pays a third party creditor under legal compulsion, on account of a debt owed by the defendant, that will discharge the defendant's liability to the creditor.[179] The claimant might then be subrogated to the position of the third party creditor (see chapter 16). Or the claimant can sue in unjust enrichment,[180] either for a full indemnity, or for a contribution. Contribution might arise at common law, when there is a common liability to the same creditor for the same debt, or under the Civil Liability (Contribution) Act 1978, when there is liability for the same damage. The 1978 Act is itself based on the principle of unjust enrichment.[181]

---

[179] *Ibrahim v Barclays Bank plc* [2012] EWCA Civ 640

[180] *Re D&D Wines International Ltd* [2016] UKSC 47, [16(4)]

Examples from the case law

- A took his carriage to B for repair. The carriage was left on B's premises. B failed to pay his rent, so landlord C took the carriage by way of distress. A had to pay the rent to recover his carriage. A could claim that rent back from B.[182]

- If a group of diners leave without paying their share, except for one person who pays for everyone, he may be able to recover from each other diner their respective share.[183]

- A tenant was served with legal notice to abate a nuisance, which he did. Later he discovered that the nuisance was due to the landlord's drains. The tenant could recover the cost from the landlord.[184]

- Solicitors A guaranteed clients B that there would be no cost risk of litigation, and arranged on their behalf insurance with C. B lost the litigation, incurring an adverse costs order. A was liable to B under its guarantee, and C was liable to B under the insurance, to meet those costs.

---

[181] *Dubai Aluminium Co Ltd v Salaam* [2002] UKHL 48, [76]

[182] *Exall v Partridge* (1799) 8 Term Rep 308

[183] *Child v Morley* (1800) 8 TR 610, 614; 101 ER 1574, 1576

[184] *Gebhardt v Saunders* [1892] 2 QB 452

A paid, and could recover 100% contribution from C, who had the primary responsibility to pay out.[185]

- The defendant imported skins and stored them in the claimant's bonded warehouse. The skins were stolen. When Customs demanded that the claimant pay the import duties, the claimant was obliged under statute to do so. The claimant could recover this from the defendant, who was primarily liable (as importer) for the import duties.[186]

- In contrast, landlord A leased property to B who assigned it to C who mortgaged it to D who took possession. When D failed to pay rent, A enforced his covenant against B. B could not then recover his payment from D. B's payment to A had not discharged any liability owed by D to A, because D was never liable to pay rent to A in the first place. D's only liability was to pay C, and that liability had not been discharged by B.[187]

---

[185] *Greene Wood McLean LLP v Templeton Insurance Ltd* [2010] EWHC 2679 (Comm)

[186] *Brook's Wharf and Bull Wharf Ltd v Goodman Bros* [1937] 1 KB 534

[187] *Bonner v Tottenham and Edmonton Permanent Investment Building Society* [1899] 1 QB 161

CHAPTER 10: PUBLIC AUTHORITIES

10.1 Payment made to a public authority, pursuant to an apparent statutory requirement, but which was not lawfully due, can be recovered by the payer.

The unjust factor was originally formulated as follows: money paid to a public authority as a tax or levy, when demanded by the public authority ultra vires (ie beyond its powers in a technical public law sense), is recoverable by the payer.[188] It was subsequently recast as follows: payment made to a public authority, pursuant to an apparent statutory requirement, but which was not lawfully due, can be recovered; there is no need for the public authority to make any demand.[189]

In contrast to mistake (see chapter 4.2), it does not matter that the claimant paid the money under protest, ie suspecting that the demand was unlawful, and so taking the risk.[190] This is because this unjust factor has a higher purpose: it seeks to protect against *unconstitutional* demands or payments. (In similar vein, money might even be recoverable from a private body whose demands exceed its statutory limits.)[191]

It may be that, because it is founded on constitutional principle, there is no change of position defence for the public authority as regards this unjust factor

---

[188] *Woolwich Equitable Building Society v IRC* [1993] AC 70

[189] *Test Claimants in the FII Group Litigation v Revenue and Customs Commissioners* [2012] UKSC 19 (*'FII Group Litigation'*)

[190] *Woolwich Equitable Building Society v IRC* [1993] AC 70

[191] *Great Western Rly Co v Sutton* (1868) LR 4 HL 226

(the defence is otherwise generally available to public authorities).[192] Also, there is no defence that repayment might cause 'fiscal chaos': it is the authority's error, and the authority should bear the burden, not the individual tax-payer.[193]

Alternative unjust factors entitling the claimant to restitution in circumstances where the public authority's demand is ultra vires might include mistake and duress. The claimant is free to choose whichever approach most suits it.[194] Thus, framing the claim in mistake might permit more generous time limits.[195] Examples of duress might include: an implicit threat to seize vehicles unless a permit fee is paid;[196] and an implicit threat not to renew a pub licence unless a fee is paid.[197]

Of course, legislation might (and often does) provide a regime which ousts or supplements the common law position.[198]

Note also a complementary principle: when a public authority acts ultra vires to make payment, it can recover that money from the payee.[199]

---

[192] *FII Group Litigation* [2008] EWHC 2893 (Ch), a point not decided on appeal at [2010] EWCA Civ 103, nor discussed on further appeal at [2012] UKSC 19; *FII Group Litigation (No 2)* [2014] EWHC 4302 (Ch), [315], reversed in part [2016] EWCA Civ 1180

[193] *Kingstreet Investments Ltd v New Brunswick (Department of Finance)* [2007] SCC 1, [25], [28]-[29]; *Woolwich Equitable Building Society v IRC* [1993] AC 70, 176

[194] *Deutsche Morgan Grenfell Group plc v IRC* [2006] UKHL 49

[195] *FII Group Litigation* [2012] UKSC 19

[196] *Mason v New South Wales* (1959) 102 CLR 108

[197] *Morgan v Palmer* (1824) 2 B & C 729, 107 ER 554

[198] Taxes Management Act 1970; Value Added Tax Act 1984

[199] *Auckland Harbour Board v R* [1924] AC 318

PART III – DEFENCES

CHAPTER 11: CHANGE OF POSITION

Change of position

11.1 It is a defence to the extent that the defendant has so changed his position as a result of the receipt that it would be inequitable to require him to make restitution.

The availability of this defence is essential to ensure balance between claimant and defendant. Remember, mistake is strict liability: the claimant can recover, even when the defendant was unaware of the mistake. A defendant who receives a payment, trusting that it is now his to spend, and so spending it, should not have to dip into his own savings to refund the claimant. In other words, the defendant is not to be treated as an insurer or guarantor against the claimant's own mistakes.

The change of position defence works proportionately (it is not an all-or-nothing defence).[200] For example, if the defendant has received £100, and spent £25, he must still repay the remaining £75. He has not changed his position in respect of the £75. Of course, if instead he had spent £100, then the defence would be total.

It is not a hardship defence. If the defendant is later made unemployed, or injured, so that he is now poorer and could do with the money, that does not change his liability to repay. In other words, the change of position must be

---

[200] *Lipkin Gorman v Karpnale Ltd* [1991] 2 AC 548

causally linked to the receipt.[201] (It was not because of the receipt that the defendant was made unemployed or became injured.)

The change of position must affect the defendant detrimentally.[202] For example, the defendant banker was promised then paid a large bonus by mistake. Refusing to return the bonus, the defendant said he had foregone the opportunity to work elsewhere. His defence was rejected. He had not proven that he would have been better off going to another employer, or that staying with this employer had been detrimental.[203]

It has been said that the defence should be available where the payment made to the defendant has been stolen from him.[204] Certainly, if money were paid to the defendant by mistake, it seems unfair to make the defendant strictly liable for its return (again, to make the defendant something like a guarantor against the consequences of the claimant's mistake). But where the defendant is to blame for having the money, for example because the defendant procured the payment through duress, then it may be fair after all for the defendant to bear the risk of the money being stolen before the court orders its return.

The defence also applies to spending money *in anticipation* of payment which is then received. So where the defendant reimbursed its agents in advance

---

[201] *Scottish Equitable plc v Derby* [2001] EWCA Civ 369; *Gale v O'Neill* [2013] EWHC 644 (Ch), [42], affirmed on appeal [2013] EWCA Civ 1554

[202] *Rover International Ltd v Cannon Film Sales Ltd (No 3)* [1989] 3 All ER 423

[203] *Commerzbank AG v Price-Jones* [2003] EWCA Civ 1663

[204] *Scottish Equitable plc v Derby* [2001] EWCA Civ 369, [30]-[31]

of receiving the claimant's (mistaken) payment, that constituted a good defence of change of position.[205]

<u>Further examples from the case law</u>

- If the claimant seeks restitution of a loan, it is no defence that the defendant has paid the loan money away to a third party. The loan would still have had to be repaid anyway. Paying it away was not in reliance upon the money being the defendant's to keep, but a risk that he would not be able to repay it when inevitably called upon.[206] (Alternatively, the defendant could take out another loan, to repay and replace the first one, leaving its overall position unchanged.)

- Customer A instructed bank B to pay C, who was A's principal. The bank did so, mistakenly thinking that cheques paid into A's account had cleared. The cheques had not cleared, and so B sought to recover the payment from C. Restitution was refused: C was contractually entitled to receive the money from A; B's payment was within its mandate; thus the payment discharged A's obligation to C, which in turn gave C a defence of change of position (by discharging A of its debt).[207]

---

[205] *Dextra Bank & Trust Co Ltd v Bank of Jamaica* [2001] UKPC 50, [38]

[206] *Goss v Chilcott* [1996] AC 788, 799; *Haugesund Kommune v Depfa ACS Bank* [2010] EWCA Civ 579

[207] *Lloyd's Bank plc v Independent Insurance Co Ltd* [2000] QB 110, 127; *Yukio Takahashi v Cheng*

- Fraudster A conned investor B into paying money into an account at bank C, which then paid the money back out to A. C knew nothing of the fraud, and had changed its position by paying the money out, as it was obliged to do under its contract with A.[208] (And C was presumably not enriched by the receipt – see chapter 2.1.)

Bad faith

11.2 The defence of change of position is not available where the defendant acts in bad faith.

It is bad faith from the outset to procure the payment through fraud (ie induced mistake). But bad faith does not require outright dishonesty; it can include acting in a way which is commercially unacceptable or which amounts to sharp practice.[209]

It is probably bad faith also where the defendant has procured the payment by exerting duress, undue influence or unconscionable conduct. A defence of change of position would unlikely be available for such unjust factors.

Zhen Shu [2011] HKCU 431, [37]-[40]. When payment is not within B's mandate, see: *Barclays Bank Ltd v WJ Simms, Son and Cooke (Southern) Ltd* [1980] QB 677

[208] *Jeremy D Stone Consultants Ltd v National Westminster Bank plc* [2013] EWHC 208 (Ch), [244]-[246]; see too *Challinor v Juliet Bellis & Co* [2015] EWCA Civ 59

[209] *Niru Battery Manufacturing Co v Milestone Trading Ltd* [2002] EWHC 1425 (Comm), [135], affirmed on appeal at [2003] EWCA Civ 1446, [164]

It is bad faith to pay away the money knowing of the facts entitling the claimant to restitution.[210] Actual knowledge might include wilfully or recklessly failing to make appropriate inquiries,[211] or deliberately turning a blind eye.[212] Similarly, if the defendant has doubts about the propriety of his receipt, the question of whether he acted in good faith might turn on what further inquiries might reasonably have been expected of him.[213]

If the change of position involves illegal conduct, this too may preclude the defence.[214] (And there is the separate defence of illegality – see chapter 12.)

Further examples from the case law

- The defendant bought a car at auction. By mistake, the private number plate was also transferred to him. Knowing of the mistake, nevertheless the defendant transferred the car and number plate to his partner. He could not rely upon a change of position defence.[215]

---

[210] *Lipkin Gorman v Karpnale Ltd* [1991] 2 AC 548, 580

[211] *Papamichael v National Westminster Bank plc* [2003] EWHC 164 (Comm), [209]

[212] *Kakavas v Crown Melbourne Ltd* (2013) 87 ALJR 708

[213] *Niru Battery Manufacturing Co v Milestone Trading Ltd* [2002] EWHC 1425 (Comm), [135], affirmed on appeal at [2003] EWCA Civ 1446, [164]; see too *Jones v Churcher* [2009] EWHC 722 (QB); *O'Neil v Gale* [2013] EWHC 644 (Ch), affirmed on appeal [2013] EWCA Civ 1554; *Abou-Rahmah v Abacha* [2006] EWCA Civ 1492; *Re Hampton Capital Ltd* [2015] EWHC 1905 (Ch); *Globenet Droid Ltd v Hong Kong Hang Lung Electronic Co* [2016] HKCU 1559 (DC)

[214] *Barros Mattos Jnr v General Securities & Finance Ltd* [2004] EWHC 1188 (Ch); *O'Neil v Gale* [2013] EWHC 644 (Ch), affirmed on appeal [2013] EWCA Civ 1554

- The defendant charged kindergarten fees illegally above the rate allowed by the Hong Kong Education Bureau. The claimant paid without knowing, having been misled by the defendant. The claimant sought to recover the excess. The defendant claimed to have spent the money on the kindergarten. This was doubted. Anyway, the defence was rejected because the defendant had acted in bad faith, given that it actively misled the claimant, and given that the defendant knew it was illegal to charge so much.[216]

---

[215] *Cressman v Coys of Kensington* [2004] EWCA Civ 47

[216] *Gloria Kindergarten v Ching Hong Yuen* [2001] HKCU 1218, [23]

Estoppel

The defendant might have a defence of estoppel where he has detrimentally relied on a representation by the claimant that the receipt was his to keep.

Such estoppel usually requires: a representation by the claimant, express, or implied (for example, because the claimant owed the defendant some duty of accuracy); that the correct amount of money had been paid over; which representation had been relied upon, in good faith, by the defendant, to his detriment, such that it would be inequitable to require him to make restitution.

<u>Examples from the case law</u>

- A soldier was paid more money upon demobilisation than he was entitled to. He did not know it was too much. By the time the error was identified, he had lost the extra money in a bad investment. The claimant was estopped from alleging the mistaken payment.[217]

- A endorsed a bill of exchange to B who endorsed it to C. C told B that the bill had cleared, and gave B a cheque, which B passed to A. In fact the bill had not cleared. When C sought to recover the amount of the cheque from B, it was estopped from doing so.[218]

---

[217] *Holt v Markham* [1923] 1 KB 504

[218] *Deutsche Bank v Beriro & Co* (1895) 73 LT 669

- In contrast, the defendant was told by his bank that he had more money in his account than was actually the case. He spent the whole sum buying a hotel. When the bank sought to recover the excess, there was no estoppel: the hotel was a good investment, and the defendant would have bought it anyway.[219]

Traditionally, estoppel was an all-or-nothing defence, but that position has been eroded:

In *Avon County Council v Howlett*,[220] estoppel was upheld as an all-or-nothing defence. But Eveleigh LJ said that there may be circumstances which would render it unconscionable for the defendant to retain an unspent balance in his hands.

In *Scottish Equitable plc v Derby*,[221] Walker LJ suggested that if the claimant limited his claim to the unspent part of what the defendant received, then there might be no detrimental reliance by the defendant in respect of that sum (ie the all-or-nothing defence could be side-stepped by a pro rata claim).

More generally, in *Scottish Equitable plc v Derby*, estoppel was seen as a relic, and any resort to its all-or-nothing approach was strongly disapproved of.[222] Instead, the court preferred the defence of change of position.[223]

---

[219] *United Overseas Bank v Jiwani* [1977] 1 All ER 733

[220] [1983] 1 All ER 1073, 1078

[221] [2001] EWCA Civ 369, [46]-[47]

[222] [2001] EWCA Civ 369, [38]-[49]

[223] See too: *Philip Collins Ltd v Davis* [2000] 3 All ER 808; *Secretary for Justice v Kwan Sin Sang*

In that case, the claimant overpaid the defendant's pension by mistake. The defendant spent some on lifestyle; the claimant could not recover that amount – the defendant had changed his position. The defendant spent some on paying off the mortgage; that was recoverable, because paying off a loan does not count as a change of position.[224] The defendant spent the rest on a new pension, which the provider was willing to unwind, and which the defendant accordingly had to repay.

In *National Westminster Bank plc v Somer International (UK) Ltd*,[225] it was held that equity required a recipient to rely on estoppel only to the extent of their detriment.

So in practice, it seems that estoppel is verging on the redundant. Its all-or-nothing nature is blunt and often indefensible, and yet a proportionate defence is precisely what change of position is (and without the additional requirement of needing a representation).

[2008] 6 HKC 203, [42]-[48]

[224] Repaying the mortgage was something which had to be done anyway regardless of the receipt. Alternatively, the defendant could take out another mortgage to repay the receipt, leaving his original position unchanged.

[225] [2001] EWCA Civ 970

CHAPTER 12: ILLEGALITY

The defence has recently been the subject of scrutiny by the Supreme Court in *Patel v Mirza*.[226] Before turning to that case, we need to understand the historical position.

The default position was that the court would not lend its aid to a person who founded their cause of action upon an illegal or immoral act.[227] But this was subject a wide range of exceptions, which made for unpredictable law.

Thus, a claim might lie where the claimant could invoke his 'locus poenitentiae', which latterly meant simply that he had withdrawn from the illegal activity before it had been carried out.[228] Or a claim might lie where the claimant was innocent of, or the defendant was to blame for, the illegality; for example, where the defendant's agent fraudulently misrepresented that the transaction was legal.[229]

Also, a claim might lie where a transaction was rendered illegal by legislation for the purposes of protecting from exploitation a class of persons, and the claimant fell within that class.[230] Or where the illegality was incidental to the

---

[226] [2016] UKSC 42

[227] *Holman v Johnson* (1775) 1 Cowp 341, 343; 98 ER 1120, 1121

[228] *Tribe v Tribe* [1996] Ch 107

[229] *Hughes v Liverpool Victoria Friendly Society* [1916] 2 KB 482

[230] *Andayani v Chan Oi Ling* [2001] 1 HKC 252; *Estinah v Golden Hand Indonesian Employment Agency* [2001] 4 HKC 607

transaction,[231] like a contract concluded in an illegally parked car.[232] Or where the claim could be made out without having to rely on the illegality.[233]

In *Patel v Mirza*, the claimant paid money to the defendant to bet on share movements with insider information. That was illegal. As it happened, the insider information was never forthcoming. The claimant sought to recover its money, successfully.

In the Supreme Court, there was seemingly consensus on the reasons why the law recognised a plea of illegality. First, no-one should profit from their own wrongdoing. Second, the law should be consistent, and not self-defeating. So for example, if criminal law proscribes certain behaviour, it should not be possible to sue in contract law for payment for the same behaviour. We might say, a thief should not be able to sue for his share of the heist.

However, there was a division of judicial opinion on how to achieve those aims.

The majority proceeded as follows:[234]

In arriving at a decision whether or not to grant the claimant a remedy, it is necessary to consider: (a) the underlying purpose of the prohibition which has

---

[231] *ParkingEye Ltd v Somerfield Stores Ltd* [2012] EWCA Civ 1338

[232] An example adapted from Heydon 1970: 171

[233] *Tinsley v Milligan* [1994] 1 AC 340

[234] Lord Toulson, Lady Hale, Lord Kerr, Lord Wilson, and Lord Hodge. Lord Neuberger also expressed agreement – except that he approached the matter from a different angle, and the minority also claimed to find support in his judgment.

been transgressed; (b) other public policies which may be rendered less effective by denial of the claim; (c) the proportionality of denying the claim.

Proportionality, they said, includes the following factors: the seriousness of the illegal behaviour; its centrality to the transaction; whether it was intentional; whether there was a marked disparity in the parties' respective culpability.

The minority approached it this way:[235]

A claim should be barred where the person making the claim has to rely in support on their illegal act; or, to put it another way, where their legal rights derive from the illegal act.

But there are exceptions. One is where the claimant's illegal act is involuntary, or the parties are not on the same footing, for example because it was brought about by the defendant's duress or fraud. Another is where applying the illegality rule would itself render the law self-defeating, for example because the proscribed behaviour was meant to protect the claimant, not further deny him a remedy.

Otherwise, they said, claimants should not be deprived of opportunity: to obtain damages for wrongs; or to put themselves in the position in which they should have been.

As for restitution, the usual position is that a claimant does not have to rely on the illegality to ground his right to repayment. The illegality renders the contract unenforceable; which explains why there has been a failure of basis. At which point, restitution of payment should follow as a matter of course. This

---

[235] Lord Mance, Lord Clarke, and Lord Sumption

returns the claimant to their original position, the position which they should have been in (ie a law-abiding position, before the illegal contract was entered into).

In other words, the right to restitution is grounded on failure of basis, ie no change from the original legal position, rather than upon new rights created by the illegality.

However, they added, this does not allow a claim for restitution which is 'functionally indistinguishable' from enforcement of contract. So for example, if a loan is rendered unenforceable by statute, the lender should not be able to side-step and recover the money in unjust enrichment (instead of contract).[236]

In the present case, they said, the claimant would not have been able to sue upon the illegal contract; but with that contract set aside, he could recover his payment.

Thus the minority's preferred approach was, again, to state a default rule, with various exceptions. The majority position was criticised for involving discretionary value judgments about what type of transactions ought to be enforced. For example, the question, whether allowing the claim would render the law self-defeating, was not, they said, merely one relevant consideration, but *the* reason for recognising the principle of illegality in the first place.

We might consider one final example from the case law, which received endorsement in *Patel v Mirza*.

A Somali claimant agreed with defendant solicitors to refer asylum seekers to them, and carry out translation work, in return for half the fees earned

---

[236] *Kusumu v Baba-Egbe* [1956] AC 539; *Barons Finance Ltd v Makanju* [2013] EWHC 153 (Ch)

114

from Legal Aid. That was an illegal agreement, and so unenforceable, as the defendant probably knew; but not the claimant, who could therefore recover the value of his work.[237]

---

[237] *Mohamed v Alaga & Co* [1999] 3 All ER 699; endorsed in *Patel v Mirza* [2016] UKSC 42, [119]

CHAPTER 13: SET-OFF & COUNTER-RESTITUTION

Set-off is a general principle (rather than something unique to unjust enrichment). For example, where a claimant has a claim for £X, and a defendant has a counterclaim for £Y, rather than have both the claim and the counterclaim paid separately and in full, instead only the balance of £(X-Y) may have to be paid. In other words, the defendant can set-off his counterclaim for £Y against the claimant's claim for £X.

In the law of unjust enrichment, it is often the case that, if a claimant is to get back what he gave to the defendant, he must also give back what he received from the defendant. So for example, if the claimant pays for and receives goods, but now wants his money back, then he must return the goods. He cannot keep the goods and recover the money.

Giving back what a claimant received is sometimes called making 'counter-restitution'. Further, it is sometimes said that a claimant's inability to give counter-restitution is a defence.[238] But why? Because, so the argument goes, otherwise the claimant himself will end up unjustly enriched (for example, if he has both the goods and his money). But that explanation, of course, depends on proving against him a counterclaim of unjust enrichment. So really it is not a defence, but an example of set-off: the defendant's counterclaim, if any, cancels out the claim.

---

[238] Burrows 2011: 569. Similarly, inability to give counter-restitution is often considered a bar to rescission of a contract – but I have argued against that position: 'Separating Rescission and Restitution' (2016) 33 Journal of Contract Law 135.

Just because a claimant has received something from the defendant, it does not mean that the defendant can raise a counterclaim in every case. For a start, the claimant might subjectively devalue anything he received, even to zero (see chapter 2.3). Or the counterclaim might be met with another defence, like change of position (see chapter 11).

<u>Examples from the case law</u>

- A pop star thought he was earning too little money, with too much going to his manager. The singer could rescind his management contract, for undue influence, and get an account of profits. But the singer was required to credit his manager with a reasonable remuneration, including a small profit element, to reflect the manager's efforts which had contributed to the singer's success.[239]

- A claimant could rescind, for misrepresentation, a contract to buy an island with a mine, and recover its payment, even having worked the mine. But it had to return the island, give an account of profits from the mining, and give an allowance for deterioration of the property.[240]

---

[239] *O'Sullivan v Management Agency & Music Ltd* [1985] QB 428; see too *Mahoney v Purnell* [1996] 3 All ER 61. Any counterclaim by the manager could have been on the basis of mistake (thinking he had a binding contract to be paid for his efforts) or failure of basis (doing all the promotion and getting nothing in return).

[240] *Erlanger v New Sombrero Phosphate Co* (1878) LR 3 App Cas 1218. It may be that the island

- In contrast,[241] the defendant was a company director who engaged in forgery, false evidence and unconscionable conduct to frustrate the claimant liquidators investigating the company's affairs. At the eleventh hour, before the deadline for implementing a scheme of arrangement, the claimant had no choice but to enter a settlement agreement with the defendant. That could later be set aside. It was no objection that the defendant could not be returned to his previous position. After all, his previous position was an unconscionable attempt to thwart the scheme of arrangement.

---

owners could frame a counterclaim in unjust enrichment on the grounds of mistake or failure of basis. But more realistically, this looks like restitutionary damages in tort: with the contract rescinded, the claimant had no right to be on the island, thus making it a trespasser in retrospect. In this vein, see too: *Ministry of Defence v Ashman* [1993] 2 EGLR 102; *Ministry of Defence v Thompson* [1993] 2 EGLR 107; *Inverugie Investments Ltd v Hackett* [1995] 1 WLR 713 (all cases of restitutionary damages for trespass to land); and *Strand Electric and Engineering Co Ltd v Brisford Entertainments Ltd* [1952] 2 QB 246 (restitutionary damages for interference with goods).

[241] *Borelli v Ting* [2010] UKPC 21. This case is best understood as follows. First, the settlement could be set aside for unconscionable conduct. Second, there was no counterclaim: there was no basis on which the claimant was *unjustly* enriched by the defendant being unable to resume his reprehensible behaviour; alternatively, any counterclaim could be met by a defence of illegality (on account of his fraud).

PART IV – CONTROVERSIES

CHAPTER 14: ENTITLEMENT

Consider the following example.

Pursuant to a contract, A delivers goods to B on credit. B owes £100. B later pays £100. But B paid this by mistake (he meant to pay someone else instead). Surely B should not be able to recover the money from A.[242]

So the first edition of this book stated the following principle:

- There can be no restitution where the defendant is legally entitled to the receipt.

Such a principle is consistent with scholarly discussion:

For example, Virgo talks about a 'legally effective basis' which bars a claim in unjust enrichment.[243] Burrows talks about legal entitlement being a 'qualification' such that enrichment is not overall unjust.[244] Tettenborn,[245] and the editors of *Goff & Jones*,[246] discuss 'justifying grounds' which give the defendant a legal entitlement to keep what he has received despite unjust enrichment otherwise being made out. Similarly, Edelman and Bant talk about 'negating juristic reasons'.[247]

---

[242] *Fairfield Sentry Ltd v Migani* [2014] UKPC 9, [18]

[243] Virgo 2015: ch 7

[244] Burrows 2011: 88-89

[245] Tettenborn 2002: 20-31

[246] Mitchel et al 2016: Pt 2

Such a principle also finds support in the case law:

For example, the courts have held that there is no obligation to make restitution where money is paid under a 'legally effective transaction';[248] a payee cannot be said to be unjustly enriched if he was 'entitled to receive' the sum paid to him;[249] there can be no unjust enrichment where payments are made pursuant to a 'valid contract' which is fully or partly performed;[250] money paid under a binding contract is not recoverable in restitution until the contract is avoided;[251] there can be no recovery of mistaken payments if the money was paid for 'good consideration';[252] a claimant cannot claim a restitutionary payment where a price is already fixed on terms by a contract.[253]

Further, the notion of entitlement is not limited to contractual entitlement: it might apply where the payment is made pursuant to a judgment;[254] or perhaps

---

[247] Edelman and Bant 2016: ch 7

[248] *Portman Building Society v Hamlyn Taylor Neck* [1998] 4 All ER 202, 208

[249] *Kleinwort Benson Ltd v Lincoln City Council* [1999] 2 AC 349, 408

[250] *Madoff Securities International Ltd v Raven* [2013] EWHC 3147 (Comm), [376]

[251] *The Evia Luck* [1992] 2 AC 152, 165

[252] *Barclays Bank Ltd v WJ Simms, Son and Cooke (Southern) Ltd* [1980] QB 677, 695; *Yukio Takahashi v Cheng Zhen Shu* (2011) 14 HKCFAR 558, [38]-[39]; *Lloyd's Bank plc v Independent Insurance Co Ltd* [2000] QB 110, 130, 132; *Jones v Churcher* [2009] EWHC 722, [41]-[42], [48]

[253] *The Olanda* [1919] 2 KB 728; *Re Richmond Gate Property Co Ltd* [1964] 3 All ER 936; *Cutter v Powell* (1795) 6 TR 320, 101 ER 573; *Sumpter v Hedges* [1898] 1 QB 673; *Benedetti v Sawiris* [2013] UKSC 50, [91]

[254] *Marriot v Hampton* (1797) 7 TR 269, 101 ER 969; *Minshall v Revenue and Customs Commissioners* [2015] EWCA Civ 741

even where receipt (by the tax authorities) is authorised under a statutory tax regime.[255]

The outcome seems right. But the method? On reflection, there do not appear to be any independent reasons for recognising a defence of entitlement, beyond mere fiat. Why does a contract, or a judgment, trump a claim in unjust enrichment? An acceptable answer cannot simply be: because it does.

True enough, in simple language it makes sense to say that the receipt is not unjust when the recipient was entitled to it. But the law of unjust enrichment does not provide a remedy simply in response to broad-brush moral sentiment. It is technical and principled. It asks: was the defendant enriched, at the expense of the claimant, through a recognised factor. There is no additional question of whether, despite all that, the overall receipt is unjust.

My view now is that there is no need for a defence of entitlement. The correct result can be achieved by other means.

Returning to the opening example:

First, A has a defence of change of position (see chapter 11). With payment accepted, the contract is fulfilled. No longer can A sue for payment. It would then be inequitable for B to recover the money, leaving A with neither the contractual right to sue, nor the money which bought out that contractual right to sue.[256]

---

[255] *Test Claimants in the Franked Investment Income Litigation v Revenue and Customs Commissioners* [2010] EWCA Civ 103, [179]-[183], not discussed on appeal at [2012] UKSC 19; but see *Deutsche Morgan Grenfell plc v Inland Revenue Commissioners* [2006] UKHL 49

[256] *Lloyd's Bank plc v Independent Insurance Co Ltd* [2000] QB 110, 126; *Yukio Takahashi v Cheng*

Second, A is not enriched. Yes, he has received money. But this is cancelled out in one of two ways (as we saw in chapter 2):

(1) We can say that A has given consideration in return. In other words, he has swapped the money for the goods. (It could have been services. Or perhaps an enforceable promise.) His net position is unchanged.

Further, B cannot say that A remains enriched on account of some supposed disparity between the money and the consideration. This is because contract law will not embark on any exercise which judges the adequacy of consideration.[257] In other words, it assumes that consideration is adequate to the price. Alternatively, the fact that B agreed the contract price would estopp him from denying the adequacy.

(2) As Edelman and Bant originally put it,[258] we might say that a person in A's position is never enriched because he merely exchanges one asset (the contractual right to payment) for another asset (the payment itself). Similarly, a bank is not enriched when it receives money for the account of one of its clients, because that receipt is matched by a liability to pay the money back out to the client.[259]

Third, rarely will there be any unjust factor. Duress, undue influence, unconscionable bargain, mistake (induced by misrepresentation) will all set aside a

Zhen Shu (2011) 14 HKCFAR 558, [39]

[257] *Chappell & Co Ltd v Nestle Co Ltd* [1960] AC 87

[258] Edelman and Bant 2006: 345

[259] *Jeremy D Stone Consultants Ltd v National Westminster Bank plc* [2013] EWHC 208 (Ch); *Challinor v Juliet Bellis & Co* [2015] EWCA Civ 59

contract. Failure of basis is a repudiatory breach which allows termination. Which means that, if the contract is still in place, then these unjust factors have not been made out. The only residuum is unilateral mistake insufficient to void a contract – but then the arguments about change of position and enrichment still apply, and the defendant might also have a contractual counterclaim.

So if a claimant wishes to be successful, then he must set aside the contract (or the judgment). In which case, the defendant could not invoke a defence of change of position: if the contract is set aside, for that reason he legitimately loses his contractual right to sue, and not consequent to the claimant's payment. And it would mean that the defendant was enriched after all, receiving the money without giving up in exchange any contractual right to it, because he no longer has any such contractual right to give up.

This approach is consistent with the case law set out above. It also explains why it has been recognized in the case law that, before a claimant can bring a claim in unjust enrichment, he must first disable any contract with the defendant which applies to the transaction,[260] or perhaps at least disable the severable part of the contract which applies to the transaction.[261] (And to be clear,

---

[260] 'To rely on total failure of consideration, the innocent party must clearly and unequivocally communicate its acceptance of the repudiation to the other party': *Fook Lee Holdings Ltd v Joy Future International Ltd* [2012] HKCU 897, [140]. Whereas affirmation of a contract precludes restitution: *Kwei Tek Chao v British Traders and Shippers Ltd* [1954] 2 QB 459.

[261] *Roxborough v Rothmans of Pall Mall Australia Ltd* (2001) 208 CLR 516; *Guido Van Der Garde BV v Force India Formula One Team Ltd* [2010] EWHC 2373 (QB)

exactly the same analysis applies when the payment is received pursuant to a judgment.)

So to summarize:

Where a defendant receives payment under a contract or judgment, there is no need to invent a defence of entitlement. Rather, the defendant will be able to argue: that he is not enriched by the receipt; or that he has a defence of change of position. This is assuming that an unjust factor can even be identified, which will be unlikely if there remains a subsisting contract (or judgment).

CHAPTER 15: NECESSITY

Take the following example: A rescues B from a state of peril or necessity. Can A recover money from B for the rescue?

To do so in unjust enrichment, the proposed unjust factor would be 'necessity'. Necessity has not been expressly recognized by the courts as an unjust factor.[262] There are some decisions which can be taken as hostile to it, and some decisions which can be taken as favourable to it. The favourable decisions tend to be pockets of cases, mostly historic, from disparate areas of law dealing with such miscellaneous topics as: burial, salvage, agency of necessity, necessaries supplied to a minor or insane person, medical care provided to paupers, necessitous payment of another's debt, and necessitous services rendered by a liquidator. Some authors argue that necessity as an unjust factor can draw support from these miscellaneous cases,[263] but this is not a unanimous view.[264]

Not all those pockets of case law do support the recognition of necessity as an unjust factor. Take salvage, for example: ship A rescues ship B in distress. In the absence of any contract between the parties, the law does indeed allow A to be paid for the rescue. However, the entitlement to payment for salvage is now set upon a statutory footing,[265] and is not pleaded as a claim in unjust enrichment.

---

[262] Although *ENE Kos 1 Ltd v Petroleo Brasileiro SA (No 2)* [2012] UKSC 17, [31] suggests the matter is still open for debate

[263] Burrows 2011: ch 18; Virgo 2015: ch 12

[264] Tettenborn 2002: ch 9; Kortmann 2005: ch 12

[265] International Convention on Salvage 1989, schedule 11 to the Merchant Shipping Act 1995

Whatever parallels salvage might have with unjust enrichment on the ground of necessity, it does not employ the language of unjust enrichment. Further, the salvage must be successful, and the payment contains a reward element, neither elements being part of the general law of unjust enrichment.

In fact, the reward and success elements of salvage are intertwined. Assume that salvage law requires the salvage to be successful before an award is made, but that the award only compensates the salvor for his costs without any reward element. If the salvage attempt is unsuccessful, the salvor will make a loss. If the salvage attempt is successful, he will not make a loss. But the losses from other unsuccessful attempts will continue to mount up. Either the salvor is driven out of business, or he only attends those vessels where success is likely. So if salvage of all vessels in distress is to be encouraged, and if there is to be a requirement of success, then there must be a reward element to balance out the lost costs of unsuccessful salvage attempts. This is implicitly reflected in the criteria for assessing a salvage award, criteria which include the state of readiness and efficiency of the salvor's equipment (ie the award must help cover the fixed costs of being a salvor who is only successful some of the time).

More generally, even if success were not to be a formal requirement for restitution in cases of rescue or necessity, still success would continue to be relevant in two ways.

First, if a rescuer is to recover anything at all, it is surely only for his *reasonable* efforts. In some circumstances, success is the only outcome of using reasonable efforts.[266]

Second, if an attempt is not successful then the person assisted might subjectively devalue his benefit. In the absence of success, it might not be possible to say that the rescue bestowed upon the person assisted an incontrovertible benefit. And without a benefit or enrichment, there is no unjust enrichment to reverse. Similarly, it might be said that the person assisted is not enriched if the value of any property preserved by the rescue is outweighed by the costs of intervention.[267]

Nevertheless, should necessity be recognized as an unjust factor as a matter of principle?

Virgo says that the necessity interferes with the claimant's free choice.[268] Presumably the point is that the rescuer would rather have walked on by. But we might make two comments here.

First, this means that only an unwilling rescuer gets paid. A kind person who freely chooses to help does not get paid. Such a law does not map well onto notions of moral deserts.

Second, the rescuer is not legally obliged to intervene. It is only his conscience that interferes with his free choice. Why is the person assisted *unjustly* enriched by the rescuer acting upon his own conscience? Why is paying money the appropriate response to an act of conscience? As Burrows says, does this mean that every charitable donation, given reluctantly but to appease one's conscience, is subsequently recoverable once the donor's attitudes harden?[269]

---

[266] Kortmann 2005: 179

[267] Burrows 2011: 484 n 99

[268] Virgo 2015: 291-292

Burrows,[270] and Virgo,[271] also say that recognizing necessity would further a policy of encouraging people to intervene to preserve the health or property of others. In other words, people might be discouraged from intervening by the financial costs of doing so. But here precisely is the problem with recognizing necessity as an unjust factor:

Unjust enrichment is not about compensating the claimant for his loss. Instead, unjust enrichment is about disgorging the defendant's gain. But there may well be times when the defendant's gain is less than the claimant's loss. In which case, the rescuer would remain out of pocket, and thus discouraged from intervening – at which point the very reason for recognizing necessity as an unjust factor is defeated.

For example, assume that the claimant drives the injured defendant to hospital. An ambulance service is usually available for free – so how could the claimant recover its out of pocket expenses? And what if the defendant cannot afford to pay? Is the defendant to be made bankrupt because of the claimant's rescue?

Or assume that a storm damages the defendant's roof. The defendant is away on holiday. The claimant replaces the tiles to stop water damage. The value of the enrichment might be assessed objectively as the cost of the tiles and the cost of a tiler. But what if the claimant did the work himself? What if he slipped and broke his arm? Can he recover for that? Or for lost income due to time off work?

---

[269] Burrows 2011: 479

[270] Burrows 2011: 480

[271] Virgo 2015: 291

What if the defendant does not like the tiles? Or the claimant has not done a good job? Or if the work needs to be re-done by a professional? What if the defendant would have suffered the water damage, or done the work himself, because he did not have enough money to pay for repairs?

If the claimant must be safeguarded financially, then a better approach is probably as follows.

First, when it comes to rescuing property, that is currently governed by the law of salvage. The courts had the opportunity to extend salvage beyond property at sea, but expressly chose not to.[272] Of course, that could still be extended by statute.

Second, when it comes to rescuing people, it might be appropriate to pay a claimant out of public funds. After all, if it is public policy to encourage intervention, then paying for it from public funds provides a satisfying symmetry. That would also require a statutory scheme.

Such a statutory scheme could avoid questions of subjective devaluation, and thus free itself of any need for the intervention to be successful. And it could ensure that the claimant is never left out of pocket, without doctrinal objections that this looks more like compensation than restitution. Such a model already exists in English law: a maritime salvor who saves lives only (rather than lives and property) cannot seek payment from the people rescued, but he can seek payment from public funds.[273]

---

[272] *The Goring* [1988] AC 831

[273] Article 16 of the International Convention on Salvage 1989 in Part I, and article 5 of Part II, of Schedule 11 to the Merchant Shipping Act 1995

To effect all this would require legislation. In its absence, necessity should not be recognized as an unjust factor, because it fits ill with the recognized principles of unjust enrichment.

CHAPTER 16: PROPERTY

This final chapter brings together a number of inter-linked controversies which go to the relationship between unjust enrichment and property law, in particular: whether ignorance should be recognized as an unjust factor; and whether unjust enrichment might yield proprietary remedies. The answer should be 'no'.

Ignorance

Ignorance has not been expressly recognized by the courts as an unjust factor. Indeed, there is some case law against its recognition.[274]

Yet there are said to be pockets of case law which can be re-interpreted as supportive of recognizing ignorance as an unjust factor. Mostly, that re-interpretation also depends on tracing (see below) and leapfrogging (see chapter 3) both being available in unjust enrichment, and the better view is that they are not.

Nevertheless, should ignorance be recognized as an unjust factor as a matter of principle? Burrows argues in favour of its recognition from the following four examples:[275]

---

[274] *Pitt v Holt* [2013] UKSC 26, [108]; *Chu Wen Jing Jennifer v Sin Hon Wai* [2016] HKCU 2745; *Globenet Droid Ltd v Hong Kong Hang Lung Electronic Co* [2016] HKCU 1559 (DC). And in *Rowe v Vale of White Horse DC* [2003] EWHC 388 (Admin), [14], the claimant's ignorance of its right to charge for sewerage services provided no ground for restitutionary payment for those services.

[275] Burrows 2011: ch 16

(i)   The claimant pays the defendant £100 by mistake;

(ii)   The claimant's computer, because of a malfunction, pays the defendant, without the claimant's knowledge, £100 twice over;

(iii)   The claimant loses £100 which is picked up by the defendant;

(iv)   The defendant steals £100 from the claimant without the claimant's knowledge.

Burrows says that, as the law is willing to give a personal restitutionary remedy in the first example, it should be willing to do so – it is illogical not to do so – in the other examples as well. In each case, he says, the claimant did not mean the defendant to have the money, and the claimant's consent was impaired or absent, and it is clear that the defendant's gain was at the expense of the claimant.

But there are problems with this approach.

In the first example, the claimant can recover in unjust enrichment. The unjust factor is *mistake*. Of course, mistake involves ignorance of the truth. So recognizing ignorance as an unjust factor would subsume mistake. Yet no-one seems to advocate that, which is rather telling. (Would ignorance of law, like mistake of law, ground a claim in unjust enrichment?)

In the second example, the claimant can probably still recover in unjust enrichment.[276] The computer is simply a tool, and its malfunction can be attributed as a mistake to its operator.

---

[276] *Barclays Bank Ltd v WJ Simms, Son and Cooke (Southern) Ltd* [1980] QB 677, 697; Tettenborn 2002: 14

In the third and fourth examples, the claimant can bring a claim, for example in tort, based upon his property in the money.[277] Burrows acknowledges that many of the cases he relies on in support of recognizing ignorance as an unjust factor are primarily reasoned in terms of interference with the claimant's ownership.[278]

So the law already provides remedies in all four examples. Just because it provides one type of remedy in one case, it does not follow that it should provide the same type of remedy in all cases. Let alone that that one remedy should be in unjust enrichment. Yes, at a high level of generality, all examples involve some sort of impaired consent. But there are factual differences too in each of the examples, and it is appropriate for the law to respond to those differences with tailored remedies.

Let us start again. Why is it unjust that the defendant profit from the claimant's ignorance? Is it wrong to profit from superior knowledge? Is that not the premise behind market economics? Is knowledge not something we are encouraged to obtain through learning?

Ignorance is not the only unjust factor Burrows argues for. He also wants powerlessness, too-busy-ness and laziness. For example, if the defendant takes the claimant's money, the claimant should be able to recover it, he says, whether the claimant was ignorant of the defendant's theft, or powerless to stop it, or too busy or too lazy to take action. Now all that is true, but the claimant's recourse is through property law, not unjust enrichment.

---

[277] See *Clerk & Lindsell* at [17-37]; Fox 1996

[278] Burrows 2011: 404-405

Again, why is it unjust that a defendant profit from the claimant being too busy or too lazy? (Powerlessness is already addressed through other recognized unjust factors such as duress or undue influence or unconscionable conduct.) But it is only ignorance plus powerlessness plus laziness plus too-busy-ness which gives Burrows the full coverage he wants. The real unjust factor he is after is 'lack of consent'.[279] And this is what the editors of *Goff & Jones* call it too.[280]

It is not every lack of consent which gives cause for complaint. The world champion may not consent to lose his crown, but he will lose it anyway when bettered by a challenger. As for the law, if a claimant gets injured, without his consent, still he can only sue in tort if he establishes a breached duty of care. And the present approach of unjust enrichment acknowledges that only certain types of lack of consent support a cause of action: mistake, duress and so on. It does not follow that, just because some types of lack of consent sound in unjust enrichment, all types should (including ignorance). Similarly, only certain types of promise sound in contract, and only certain types of wrong sound in tort.

What lack of consent really means, in examples three and four above, ie those examples not already covered by unjust enrichment, is 'you have my property'. So recognizing lack of consent as an unjust factor would simply have unjust enrichment overlay property law. That would double up actions unnecessarily. Birks said that there was a conceptual and practical necessity to keep those two subjects from merging into one.[281] Indeed, it confuses the

---

[279] Burrows 2011: 406 n 8

[280] Mitchel et al 2016: ch 8

[281] Birks 1989: 15

distinction between a personal restitutionary remedy ('give me the profits you made at my expense') and vindicating property rights ('give me back my property, or pay up').

Or to put matters another way, property law always requires a *thing*; the thing itself, and the rights in it, are central to property law. But unjust enrichment always starts with a *person*; it is essential to identify the defendant who has been enriched. Thus property law and unjust enrichment start from two different places, and then flow out along different conceptual routes. Factually, there might be overlap in certain circumstances. But conceptually, they are operating differently.

In summary, ignorance should not be recognized as an unjust factor. There is nothing inherently unjust with someone profiting from another's ignorance (or busy-ness or laziness). And expanding ignorance into 'lack of consent' risks a voyage into intellectually murky waters. It confuses property law, which centres on a thing misused, with unjust enrichment, which centres on a person enriched. That confusion is not justified when there is no need for it, given that property law and unjust enrichment between them, but separately, already provide sufficient remedies across the board.

Proprietary remedies

Proprietary remedies: whoever has my property (or its substitute) must give it back or pay up. Personal remedies: whoever is the 'wrongdoer' has to pay me a sum of money, for example in tort to compensate for the harm done, in contract to fulfil my disappointed expectations, and in unjust enrichment to make restitution for his unjust profit. So if A's car is stolen by B and given to C, A can pursue B for a personal remedy (for stealing the car), or C for a proprietary remedy (for having the car).

Unjust enrichment definitely results in personal remedies (ie the defendant has to pay money). And restitutionary remedies may well arise in property law. But can unjust enrichment result in proprietary remedies? The better answer is 'no', and there are a number of reasons why this should be.

First, whereas previously it was argued by some that tracing was part of the law of unjust enrichment, the courts have now confirmed that this part of property law, and not the law of unjust enrichment.[282] This in itself suggests a separation between property and unjust enrichment.

Second, we have also seen that unjust enrichment does not involve leapfrogging (see chapter 3). Thus, if A transacts with B who transacts with C, so that goods flow down the chain, A cannot leapfrog B to sue C in unjust enrichment. Now, A might be able to sue C in property law, if C has A's property. So when comparing unjust enrichment, which precludes leapfrogging, with property law,

---

[282] *Foskett v McKeown* [2001] 1 AC 102, 127; *Armstrong DLW GmbH v Winnington Networks Ltd* [2012] EWHC 10 (Ch), [95]

which allows it, we have further reason to believe that unjust enrichment should not yield proprietary remedies.

Third, even those who argue in favour of proprietary remedies accept that unjust enrichment cannot produce proprietary remedies in every instance. If the claimant loans money, unsecured, to the defendant, who fails to repay it, the claimant might well have a cause of action in unjust enrichment, the unjust factor being failure of basis (the loan is not repaid), or perhaps mistake (as to the debtor's *current* solvency). In which case, the claimant should have only a personal remedy. If instead he gets a proprietary remedy, that would convert him into a secured creditor. As Burrows says, that would destroy the law of insolvency at a stroke.[283]

So when might unjust enrichment result in proprietary remedies, as a matter of principle? Burrows' position can be summarized as follows.[284]

Proprietary restitution, he says, should only arise when the unjust factor operates from the beginning of the transaction, so that the defendant only ever obtains the property 'conditionally'. (This, he says, will be the case with transactions tainted by mistake or duress.) If instead the defendant obtains any property unconditionally, and the injustice arises later (for example, the defendant subsequently fails to perform his side of the bargain), then no proprietary remedy should be available. This is because, in the latter case, the claimant allowed the defendant to obtain the property unconditionally, and thereby took the risk of those 'unjust' circumstances arising later, and of the defendant's insolvency. The claimant should only be able to get a proprietary remedy, Burrows says, and so be

---

[283] Burrows 2011: 174

[284] Burrows 2011: 174-179

treated as if a secured creditor, where he has not taken the risk of the defendant's insolvency.

However, this approach is unattractive.

Assume, for example, that the claimant sells his car to the defendant, but now wants his car back. If the claimant seeks to sue in unjust enrichment, he must first set aside the contract of sale, otherwise the defendant would have a defence of change of position, or argue that he was not enriched (see chapter 14). So in what circumstances might the contract of sale be set aside?

If the contract is tainted by mistake, the only type of mistake which can set aside a contract does so by rendering the contract void. In which case, the contract never existed, and title never passed. The defendant did not gain 'conditional' title, but no title at all, which stayed at all times with the claimant. The claimant can recover his car, because it remains, and always was, his car.[285] This is a matter of property law.

If the contract of sale is tainted by duress (not mistake), this renders a contract voidable (so too with misrepresentation, undue influence, and unconscionable conduct). And 'full' title does pass. The defendant can deal with the car as his own, and even pass full title onto a third party, until the contract is rescinded, if at all (it might instead be affirmed). But if the contract is rescinded, it is cancelled, both future rights and past rights, as if the contract never existed. This reveals and restores an underlying previous state of affairs in property. In other words, title re-vests in the transferor, as if it had been there all along.[286] At least,

[285] *Cundy v Lindsay* (1878) 3 App Cas 459, 466

[286] *Car and Universal Finance Co Ltd v Caldwell* [1965] 1 QB 525

146

that is so for common law rescission (eg for duress). With equitable rescission (eg for undue influence or unconscionable conduct), the property might now be held on constructive trust.[287] But either way, the claimant recovers a property interest.[288]

An alternative approach in unjust enrichment is redundant, and it is difficult to see how it would work anyway. How is the defendant enriched by the possession of a car which remains the property of the claimant?[289]

One argument is that the defendant is enriched by the fact of possession: he could use the car; and factual possession gives him a legal right to defend that possession, against anyone except the true owner.[290] However:

First, if the defendant does actually use the car, then yes, he gets a benefit, and that might be something which yields a restitutionary remedy: the defendant might have to disgorge his profitable (because free) use of the car by paying hire. But (i) this is restitution, not based on unjust enrichment, but on equitable or tortious wrongdoing (ie interference with another's property);[291] and (ii) this is a personal remedy (ie money to pay for the use of the car), not a proprietary one.

---

[287] *National Crime Agency v Robb* [2014] EWHC 4384 (Ch)

[288] Rescission will not re-vest title if, in the interim, a third party has acquired rights, being a good faith purchaser for value without notice. That defence is again only applicable in property law, and is not available against a claim in unjust enrichment: *Foskett v McKeown* [2001] 1 AC 102, 129; Virgo 2015: 656

[289] Swadling 2008

[290] Mitchel et al 2016: [5-32]; Lodder 2012: 93-95; Edelman and Bant, *Unjust Enrichment*, 2nd edn (Oxford: Hart, 2016) 58-59

[291] *Strand Electric and Engineering Co Ltd v Brisford Entertainments Ltd* [1952] 2 QB 246 (CA); *Penarth Dock Engineering Co Ltd v Pounds* [1963] 1 Lloyd's Rep 359 (QBD); *Ministry of Defence v*

Second, as to the legal right to defend possession: (i) the abstract right to defend goods in one's possession is something which the defendant already possessed anyway: it is a tortious right we all have. There is no new enrichment here. (ii) Gaining a legal right to sue in a specific instance in tort is not necessarily an enrichment either. For example, a person is surely not enriched by his neighbour's nuisance, even though he can now sue. (iii) It is difficult to see why a defendant would incur the cost of defending possession if he was not going to use the car – which simply takes us back to the point that use is different from mere (unused) possession. (iv) Grantham and Rickett suggest that any tortious right to defend possession is anyway cancelled out (so no enrichment) by the tortious liability to return possession to the true owner.[292]

At which point, once again, how is the defendant enriched by the mere unused possession of something which is the claimant's property? To press the point further, imagine the claimant parks his car on the defendant's property, and the defendant does not know. Surely the defendant is not enriched by the mere (unused) presence of the car on his property.

In short, when a transaction which transfers property, tainted from the outset, is void or rescinded, property law already provides a proprietary remedy. Which makes it redundant to seek the same outcome in unjust enrichment. And anyway the defendant is not enriched by mere receipt of another's property.

Virgo says that no case has recognised that unjust enrichment gives rise to proprietary remedies. Instead, he says, unjust enrichment only leads to personal

Ashman (1993) 66 P & CR 195 (CA)

[292] Grantham and Rickett 2000: 40, 272-274

remedies.[293] This is the tidier view. It also aligns the denial of proprietary remedies with the denial that tracing has anything to do with unjust enrichment.

Constructive trust

Can a constructive trust ever be imposed to reverse unjust enrichment? The answer should be 'no', because it suffers from all the same problems which beset proprietary remedies generally in the context of unjust enrichment. But there are a couple of cases we need to consider.

In *Allcard v Skinner*,[294] the claimant made gifts to her mother superior when she became an initiate. When she later left the order, she sought to recover her gifts. The court said that she had left it too late; the gifts had been affirmed. But the court seemed to assume that, otherwise, the gifts would have been clothed with a constructive trust.

The case of *Allcard v Skinner* is often taken as supportive of the notion that a claimant can obtain a restitutionary remedy, in principle, by pleading undue influence. Unjust enrichment was not a recognized cause of action when that case was decided, but if the facts were to repeat, then it does seem that such a claimant could recover a personal restitutionary remedy (ie money to repay the value of the gifts). So where does the constructive trust come from?

The constructive trust arises because the facts of that case otherwise fit a well-entrenched principle of equity: where a gift is received by someone, to their

[293] Virgo 2015: 9, 11-12, 15-16, 559-560

[294] (1887) LR 36 Ch D 145

personal advantage, who stands in a fiduciary relationship of influence as regards the donor, the recipient holds the gift on constructive trust.[295] It is not the cause of action in unjust enrichment which gives rise to the constructive trust; rather, the constructive trust is a remedy provided for an equitable wrong.[296] A claimant in a similar position to *Allcard v Skinner* has a choice between suing in unjust enrichment, or claiming a constructive trust in equity.

Given that undue influence requires the defendant to hold a position of trust and confidence over the claimant, it may well be that, in many cases of undue influence, the alternative remedy of constructive trust is available. But it does not follow that a constructive trust will arise in respect of every other unjust factor. After all, mistake, duress, and failure of basis are all possible without the defendant being in a fiduciary position.

And yet, in *Chase Manhattan Bank NA v Israel-British Bank (London) Ltd*,[297] it was held that money paid by mistake from one bank to another was also held on constructive trust, even though the recipient bank stood in no fiduciary relationship to the transferor.

However, that result was subsequently explained as follows. In *Westdeutsche Landesbank Girozentrale v Islington LBC*,[298] Lord Wilberforce said that the constructive trust arose as a result of it being unconscionable for the recipient bank to retain the second payment once it realized the mistake. In other

---

[295] Martin 2012: [12-009]; Virgo 2015: 502-504; *Re Biss* [1903] 2 Ch 40, 58

[296] Virgo 2015: 277, ch 19

[297] [1981] Ch 105

[298] [1996] AC 669, 715

words, the constructive trust did not arise to reverse any unjust enrichment; rather, it arose in response to a separate equitable notion of unconscionable retention.[299]

In short, a constructive trust can arise following an equitable wrong, but it is not a remedy for unjust enrichment.

Subrogation

Subrogation is a complicated and multi-faceted topic covering a miscellany of cases whose interpretation is controversial. Subrogation is where, broadly speaking, A steps into the shoes of B, to take over B's rights and remedies against C. Those might be personal or proprietary remedies. Subrogation can be provided for expressly or implicitly by contract (as is commonly the case with insurance). Or subrogation can be available non-contractually. The ascendant view is that non-contractual subrogation can be available to reverse or prevent C's unjust enrichment.[300] Thus, alongside personal remedies (ie money payments), unjust enrichment might also lead to subrogation. A second view is that subrogation is primarily concerned with vindicating property rights.[301] A third view is that including subrogation within the law of restitution at all is unsatisfactory.[302]

If subrogation is used to reverse unjust enrichment, then it happens as follows. The law re-creates rights for A. It is not the case that B's rights are simply

---

[299] Virgo 2015: 598-600; Glister and Lee 2015: [26-011]

[300] *Banque Financiere de la Cite v Parc (Battersea) Ltd* [1999] 1 AC 221

[301] Virgo 2015: 21, 637

[302] Tettenborn 2002: 63-64

assigned to A, or that somehow the law 'keeps them alive'. Indeed, it is the very extinction of those rights which creates the unjust enrichment that subrogation seeks to reverse. But the law cannot re-create any old rights for A. It can only re-create the rights which B previously enjoyed. And it can then diminish those rights if otherwise A would gain a windfall, rather than a mere reversal of unjust enrichment.[303]

The leading modern account of subrogation as reversing unjust enrichment comes from *Banque Financiere de la Cite v Parc (Battersea) Ltd*.[304] In that case, Parc owed a debt to R, who had a first legal charge, and to the defendant, who had a second legal charge. Parc wanted to pay off its debt to R. It sought a loan from the claimant bank. But in order to circumvent (legally) Swiss banking law, the loan was made to H, a director of Parc's holding company, who used the loan to pay off the debt owed to R. The claimant bank wanted security for its debt, so H promised that the claimant would be repaid by Parc in priority to the defendant. This promise did not bind the defendant. Then Parc became insolvent. The court held that the claimant could be subrogated to R's position of priority over the defendant.

The court's reasoning was as follows. The defendant was enriched, in effect because it was promoted from second to first legal charge. The unjust factor was mistake, because the claimant wrongly thought it was given priority over the defendant (which was a precondition of giving the loan). The enrichment was at the expense of the claimant, directly said Lord Hoffmann, on the basis that it was

[303] Mitchel et al 2016: [39-37]-[39-48]

[304] [1999] 1 AC 221; similarly, see *Day v Tiuta International Ltd* [2014] EWCA Civ 1246

the claimant's money which promoted the defendant.[305] Similarly, Lord Steyn said that, although the interposition of H fulfilled a genuine purpose in circumventing Swiss banking rules, nevertheless the reality was that the defendant was enriched by the claimant's money, and it would be 'pure formalism' to allow the interposition of H to defeat the claim in unjust enrichment.[306]

But Burrows says that this is indirect enrichment,[307] and on this approach to the case, he must be right: the transfer of value came from H, who had taken the loan from the claimant, for genuine reasons, and was liable for its repayment. Descriptively, the defendant might have been enriched by the claimant's money, but only at a second remove, through the mediation of H, acting as principal, and that ought to break the chain of causation.

But a different analysis gets the same result without upsetting the usual rule that enrichment must be at the expense of the claimant (see chapter 3). The defendant was enriched by getting a larger distribution on Parc's insolvency (now that it had been promoted to first legal charge). This was at the expense of the claimant, an unsecured creditor who accordingly would have got a smaller distribution (as would other creditors). The unjust factor was the claimant's mistake (which is why only the claimant could sue in unjust enrichment, and not all other disappointed creditors) in believing it had priority over the defendant when it provided the loan.

---

[305] [1999] 1 AC 221, 235

[306] [1999] 1 AC 221, 227

[307] Burrows 2011: 153 n 48

Note that the claimant got a personal remedy.[308] It did not actually get a first legal charge; it simply got priority over the defendant, but not over any other creditor. In those circumstances, talk of subrogation was superfluous; in effect, the claimant simply got the money which would otherwise have been distributed in priority to the defendant. In this regard, Lord Steyn was content to decide the case primarily as a straightforward application of unjust enrichment without recourse to subrogation. Burrows too says that subrogation is unnecessary because the unjust enrichment analysis which leads to subrogation should directly trigger restitution anyway.[309]

Another case to consider is *Bank of Cyprus UK Ltd v Menelaou*.[310] In that case, a bank had lent money to parents, secured by a charge on their house. The parents sold their house. Thus the proceeds of sale should have gone to the bank to repay the loan. Instead, the parents wanted to use some of that money to buy another house for their daughter. The bank said that this was acceptable, as long as it got a replacement charge on that other house. After that other house was bought, the daughter said that she knew nothing of this arrangement, and sought to have the charge cancelled, so that she would own the house outright. Because of her ignorance, the charge over that other house was indeed invalid, but the court provided the bank with a proprietary remedy.

The reasoning was as follows. The daughter was enriched (by getting a house she did not pay for). This enrichment was at the expense of the bank (there

---

[308] Virgo 2015: 637

[309] Burrows 2011: 147, 148

[310] [2015] UKSC 66

was some discussion of this being indirect enrichment, but it is probably direct enrichment after all – see chapter 3). The unjust factor was either mistake or failure of basis (the bank advanced money but did not get the valid security it had insisted upon). The bank could get a proprietary remedy as follows. The vendor of that other house had an unpaid vendor's lien, covering the period between selling the house and being paid for it. The vendor was paid for it, but by money in effect advanced by the bank. Thus the bank's money paid off the vendor, allowing the bank to be subrogated to the vendor's position, and the lien.

In summing up the relationship between subrogation and unjust enrichment, caution is needed.

First, just because there is a cause of action in unjust enrichment, it does not follow that subrogation is available. It only arises in three party cases. There must be another position to be subrogated to.

Second, if that other position only comes with personal remedies, then subrogation can only re-create personal remedies,[311] and not invent new proprietary remedies.

Third, if that other position comes with proprietary remedies, still, the claimant cannot get full-on property rights, good against all the world. It can only get rights to prevent the personal unjust enrichment of a specific defendant.

To repeat, unjust enrichment cannot, conceptually, given the ingredients of its cause of action, start by looking at a *thing*, to decide what rights the claimant

---

[311] *Filby v Mortgage Express (No 2) Ltd* [2004] EWCA Civ 759; *Niru Battery Manufacturing Co v Milestone Trading Ltd (No 2)* [2004] EWCA Civ 487; *Re Beppler & Jacobson Ltd* [2016] EWHC 20 (Ch)

has in it, good against all the world. That is what property law does. Instead, unjust enrichment must start by identifying a *person* enriched. It is only by identifying a person enriched that the claimant is entitled to subrogation for unjust enrichment. And the rights then re-created are only those sufficient to reverse the personal enrichment of the defendant.

In *Parc*, the claimant did not get a proprietary remedy (a legal charge), but personal priority only over one defendant. In *Menelaou*, if the claimant did get a lien, it was because the lien did not bite against all the world; rather, the only person it affected was the one defendant.

OUTLINE SUMMARY

Remedies: (I.) Restitution (ie MONEY) to disgorge the defendant's enrichment (no proprietary remedies); (II.) SUBROGATION (The claimant steps into the shoes of X to take up X's rights / remedies against the defendant; *but* only to the extent of reversing the defendant's personal enrichment)

Cause of action: (1) The defendant is enriched (objective valuation – but subjective devaluation, *unless* incontrovertible benefit, *or* the defendant's behaviour shows he valued the receipt); (2) At the expense of the claimant (no leapfrogging or intervening principals); (3) Through an unjust factor:

A. Mistake (≠ risk, mis-prediction or doubt; strict liability)

B. Duress: demand, backed by threat of an unlawful act, which coerces the claimant and causes transaction (lawful act duress (?) probably requires malice too)

C. Undue influence: actual (overt, proven acts) or presumed (relationship of trust and confidence, *and* transaction calls for an explanation. The defendant can rebut by giving explanation)

D. Unconscionable conduct: special weakness, which the defendant exploits to shock conscience of court; *unless* the defendant shows fair and reasonable

E. Failure of basis: not getting what the claimant *legitimately* expected from the transaction (total or partial failure?)

F. Legal compulsion: where the claimant is legally compelled to pay X, thereby also discharging the defendant's liability to X (the defendant must pay his share)

G. Payment made to a public authority, pursuant to an apparent statutory requirement, but which was not lawfully due.

Defences: (i) Change of position (caused by the receipt, in good faith, in circumstances making it inequitable to require restitution); Estoppel? (but pro-rata estoppel is change of position); (ii) Illegality; (iii) If the claimant does not make counter-restitution, the defendant *may* have a counterclaim in unjust enrichment which he can set-off.

CITATIONS

Baker, 'The History of Quasi-Contract in English Law', in Cornish et al (eds), *Restitution: Past, Present and Future* (Oxford: Hart, 1998)

Bigwood, 'Contracts by Unfair Advantage: From Exploitation to Transactional Neglect' (2005) 25 OJLS 65

Birks, *An Introduction to the Law of Restitution* (Oxford: Clarendon Press, 1989)

----- *Unjust Enrichment*, 2nd edn (Oxford: Oxford University Press, 2005)

Burrows, *The Law of Restitution*, 3rd edn (Oxford: Oxford University Press, 2011)

Clerk & Lindsell on Tort, 21st edn (London: Sweet & Maxwell, 2014)

Chen-Wishart, 'Undue Influence: Vindicating Relationships of Influence' (2006) 59 CLP 231

Edelman and Bant, *Unjust Enrichment in Australia* (Melbourne: Oxford University Press, 2006)

----- *Unjust Enrichment*, 2nd edn (Oxford: Hart, 2016)

Fox, 'The Transfer of Legal Title to Money' [2006] Restitution Law Review 60

Glister and Lee, *Modern Equity*, 20th edn (London: Sweet & Maxwell, 2015)

Grantham and Rickett, *Enrichment and Restitution in New Zealand* (Oxford: Hart, 2000)

Heydon, 'The Defence of Justification in Cases of Intentionally Caused Economic Harm' (1970) 20 U Toronto LJ 139

Kortmann, *Altruism in Private Law* (Oxford: Oxford University Press, 2005)

Langbein, 'The Later History of Restitution', in Cornish et al (eds), *Restitution: Past, Present and Future* (Oxford: Hart, 1998)

Lodder, *Enrichment in the Law of Unjust Enrichment and Restitution* (Oxford: Hart, 2012)

Martin, *Modern Equity*, 19th edn (London: Sweet & Maxwell, 2012)

Mitchel et al (eds), *Goff & Jones: The Law of Unjust Enrichment*, 9th edn (London: Sweet & Maxwell, 2016)

Swadling, 'Ignorance and Unjust Enrichment: The Problem of Title' (2008) 28 OJLS 627

Tamblyn, 'Separating Rescission and Restitution' (2016) 33 Journal of Contract Law 135

----- *The Law of Duress and Necessity* (Routledge)

Tettenborn, *Law of Restitution in England and Ireland*, 3rd edn (London: Cavendish, 2002)

Virgo, 'Demolishing the Pyramid – Presence of Basis and Risk-Taking in the Law of Unjust Enrichment', in Robertson, Tang (eds), *The Goals of Private Law* (Oxford: Hart, 2009)

----- *The Principles of the Law of Restitution*, 3rd edn (Oxford: Oxford University Press, 2015)

Printed in Great Britain
by Amazon